'You'll Get Over It'

VIRGINIA IRONSIDE

'You'll Get Over It'

The Rage of Bereavement

HAMISH HAMILTON · LONDON

HAMISH HAMILTON LTD

Published by the Penguin Group
Penguin Books Ltd, 27 Wrights Lane, London w8 5tz, England
Penguin Books USA Inc., 375 Hudson Street, New York, New York 10014, USA
Penguin Books Australia Ltd, Ringwood, Victoria, Australia
Penguin Books Canada Ltd, 10 Alcorn Avenue, Toronto, Ontario, Canada m4v 3b2
Penguin Books (NZ) Ltd, 182–190 Wairau Road, Auckland 10, New Zealand

Penguin Books Ltd, Registered Offices: Harmondsworth, Middlesex, England

First published 1996
3 5 7 9 10 8 6 4 2

Printed in England by Clays Ltd, St Ives plc
Filmset in 11/13pt Monophoto Garamond
Set by Datix International Limited, Bungay, Suffolk

A CIP catalogue record for this book is available from the British Library
ISBN 0–241–00222–2

For

Janey and Christopher, *my two strange parents*
Phyl, *from her Toosie*
Danny, *who told me about wild flowers, and* Kum-Kum
who wasn't such an old stick as I thought at the time
Rene and Nellie Ironside, *my headmistress and*
great-aunt with a Scottish sense of duty, and her more
light-hearted sister
Robin Ironside, *painter and genius*
Kevin Macdonald, *who jumped from a roof*
Diana Holman Hunt, *whom I loved very much*
Sebastian Walker, *who died too young*
Bobby Birch, *my first boss*
Diana Lyle, *who wanted to die, and whom I still miss*
dreadfully
Jimmy Taylor, *'the first leaf off the tree'*
Delia, Miriam and Gemma, *my three little cousins who*
died in a fire
Peter Black, *who died when I was writing this book, two*
years after his wife ('She first deceased, he for a little tried/
To live without her, liked it not, and died')

without whom I would never have had to go
through all this

Contents

Introduction

Before my father died I thought I knew a bit about bereavement. And I did. A bit. I knew about the shock and the crying; I knew about feeling special, and I had also got a whiff of my own mortality. I knew, intellectually at least, about the anger people are meant to feel when they're bereaved, and in my job as an agony aunt I would blithely send out leaflets to bereaved people – leaflets which told of the stages of grief and were full of kindly, sympathetic advice.

Then my father died. And nothing made sense any more. I was in a new world, with a new language and new emotions. Perhaps he was resting in peace, but I was in utter turmoil. I was stunned, and crazy. Not with grief, which, it turned out, was only a small part of the whole ghastly process, but with other shameful feelings of rage, greed, loathing, hatred for life – and with new, surprising interests in religion and the afterlife . . .

In the same way that a relationship between two people consists of much more than just romantic love (it may not include romantic love at all) and probably includes all kinds of complications – projection, sexual attraction, emotional crutches, trust, neurotic and selfish needs – so there is a great deal more to bereavement than just grief, which is what, of course, makes it so difficult.

As one who tends to find that books offer me the most comfort, understanding and good sense, I read and I read and I read, trying desperately to understand what I was feeling. I devoured every newspaper interview with bereaved people, and read as many books on bereavement as I could. And with a few exceptions in which the authors shared their personal experience, nearly every book was written as if by an interested anthropologist about another world. Detached. Patronizing. And often, it seemed to me, dishonest.

Most of them enraged me. From each one oozed, it seemed,

a gluey sentimentality, every bit as schmaltzy as any Pre-Raphaelite picture of a woman lying prostrate on a grave. In one, the sentimentality might come as a comfort kit – advising the reader to speak to her mom as if she were in a chair, and say goodbye, or write her dead dad a letter telling him how she loved him; in another it came in sickly paeans of praise to the enriching effects of pain, as inappropriate as extolling the nutritional effects of cyanide; in another it came in the queer, flowery and sometimes almost declamatory language that bereavement brings out in people – 'Courage, sometimes, I do not have,' wrote Daphne du Maurier, when writing of her feelings about her husband's death, with all the cumbersome pomposity of a newly elected mayor. There were too many words around like 'mourning', 'healing', 'weeping', 'lamenting', 'wounds' that 'opened anew' – not to mention a lot of guff about seasons; or the sentimentality came in poems like Canon Holland's famous piece of nonsense (entitled 'Death is Nothing at All') which claims that the dead person is only in the next room and that: 'All is well.'

After my father's death I wanted to write a book that told the truth, a truth which says: All is *not* well. Bereavement is a beastly business. Or, as one man I talked to put it: 'Death stinks.'

It was only more recently that I discovered I was not the only one to feel like this. And it seemed that, perhaps as members of a Western lapsed Christian society, bereaved people are in increasing turmoil about their feelings, and, perhaps, willing to be more honest about the darker side of bereavement than they used to be.

'I found that academic studies seemed to ignore feelings and emotional responses, and that I had to go to more literary sources for any understanding of the underlying relationships,' wrote Valerie Smith recently in a moving piece included in *Death of a Mother: Daughters' Stories.*

> ... few bereavement studies take into account 'inappropriate' negative responses, except the common phrase 'a happy release' when the deceased had suffered

much pain and ill-health. In anecdotal sources, bereaved middle-aged children share my feelings of liberation into true adulthood; but such feelings of liberation are not touched on in academic works ... I would like to see research that asks questions about rage and anger, about the forbidden feelings, the unacceptable responses to death and bereavement. In learning to cope with the death of a parent, we begin to face the reality of our own mortality. It would have helped me to understand the situation better if I had been able to find fuller, more truthful accounts of the experience of mid-life bereavement. I would have felt less guilty, less ashamed.

When one is bereaved, of course it is quite natural to fume at all bereavement books and research, even, or perhaps especially, those that offer any kind of advice or comfort – two of my 'helpful' bereavement books actually bear my enraged bite-marks chewed into the covers before being flung across the room. Perhaps this book will come in for the same treatment from you. Nothing on bereavement can be right for everyone, and many unhappy people will prefer a misty-eyed collection of helpful poems (of which there are some very touching ones, and, I have to add, why not?). And while I have not, I hope, failed to put the boot in to some of the unhelpfully rigid current thinking on bereavement, it would be too cruel to give the reader the idea that books that offer comfort and help are useless. Not at all. It often depends on one's mood, anyway, whether the advice and attitudes come across as a load of rubbish, or as sensitive insights. When you're bereaved you're so all over the place that you might find a book heart-warming on a Tuesday and mindless nonsense on a Wednesday.

My credentials for writing a book on bereavement? As I have said, it was my father's death that was the trigger. But like most middle-aged people, I've been through a few bereavements – and though none has confused me anything like as much as his, his death reminded me of other feelings of confusion I had had in the past, worrying feelings, yes, but feelings that were over too quickly to look at closely.

I should probably have known there was something funny going on, because the people in my life who have died have suffered, it seemed to me, rather odd and miserable deaths. It never occurred to me that this was actually the norm. I still went along with the general view that most people pass away peacefully with a close relative near by holding their bony old hands and mouthing: 'I love you.'

But this scenario is as much of a fantasy as that bereavement is about crying and sobbing and then getting over it. The truth is that the way most people die is often pretty grim. The current thinking in the States that we should all aim for 'a good death' is a pernicious fantasy, along with ideas that relationships can be perfect, and that bereavements can be successfully 'worked through', making us bitterly disappointed when things don't work out like in the fairy stories we've been fed. (There are some bereavement books that talk, believe it or not, about 'grief work' and 'constructive grief'.)

I feel now that the correct response to someone who announces that they have recently been bereaved should not simply be 'How sad!' It should also be: 'How frightening! How frightful!'

'I never wondered what death would be like,' said one man whose brother died. 'I thought . . . well, I didn't think. I thought people just kind of fizzled out. I was completely unprepared for the horror of it all, the hospital, the machinery, the other people, all complete strangers, involved.'

My artist uncle died alone in hospital, of a heart attack brought on by an addiction to a kind of stomach medicine that at one point in the past contained opium. Because my father was so upset I had to arrange the funeral.

My much-loved grandmother died alone in a ward in St Mary Abbot's hospital, convinced that she was surrounded by strange and sinister men in pale grey top hats who had been sent to torment her in her last days.

My great-aunt died alone in hospital, certain that each night the nurses moved her into different rooms and beat her with iron bars.

But there were bigger deaths. When I was about twenty, my best friend committed suicide with an overdose of sleeping pills. I had managed to stop her once, when, on her way to a hotel in Brighton where she was going to put a 'Do not disturb' sign on the door and cram herself with pills, she popped in to say goodbye. But the second time I expect she thought she'd already said goodbye . . .

After two suicide attempts, my mother died of cancer at sixty, much to her and my relief. Or did she die of cancer? Not technically. Her death had to be 'aided' — in other words, I had to beg for the doctor to deliver her a fatal injection. Although I was with her when she fell asleep, thanking me, she, too, died alone.

An extremely close friend died of AIDS, refused all visitors as he died, and later lay, blue with death, surrounded by candles, his fashionable stubble still apparently growing.

Another wonderful friend, who had been like a mother to me, had been in acute pain for years and begged me for the address of the Voluntary Euthanasia Society. After ordering a book through them, and following the rules to the letter, she died alone with a plastic bag over her head.

And most recently my father died at seventy-nine. He was taken into hospital with a suspected thrombosis on a Thursday, found he had got leukaemia on the Saturday, was told that chemotherapy would start on the Monday, and sensibly turned his face to the hospital wall and threw in the towel, alone, on the Sunday night. It was this death that prompted the rollercoaster of unacceptable feelings that came flooding over me and set me searching for any way to get a grip on them, trawling through magazines, books and articles for any responses to death that remotely reflected my own.

About 560,000 people die each year in the UK, mostly in hospital, resulting in about one and a half million people suffering a major bereavement. Hundreds of widows and widowers are created every day. There's just no dodging it. Some years ago the medical faculty at Stanford University isolated specimens of human cell culture. The cells were given top treatment, and when they started flagging they were boosted with extra proteins, salts and vitamins. But though they perked up, the periods of recovery became shorter and shorter and the culture got feebler and feebler and finally died.

But though death is programmed into our physical bodies – death is the only absolute certainty in life – its existence does not seem to be programmed into our minds. It is a taboo subject. We are taught about sex and birth control at school (well, sometimes we are), but we are never taught anything about death or how we might feel when it happens. There is vague talk about children learning about death when their pet hamsters or goldfish die. But while the death of a child's personal dog, fed and exercised only by its owner (a highly unlikely situation as most mothers know), might convey to the child a glimmer of what it feels like to be bereaved, most of us usually arrive at our first human bereavement as adults, completely unprepared for what is to come.

So the first thing I looked at were those studies that tried to impose order on disorder. And it seems that the most we have learned about bereavement has been from very well-meaning, but often irritating, pieces of research that try to pin down the feelings of bereavement and slot them into the so-called 'stages' of grieving. ('Stages!' The very word makes the bereaved person sigh with relief. Stages sound like steps, wonderful things you can take one at a time, moving on when you are ready. What an awful disappointment is in store for the believer in stages.)

This attempt to force a pattern on bereavement, or even turn it into an emotional process, results naturally from the fear that we feel after a death. It is terribly important for us to get everything into neat categories and then to get our emotions into the 'right' order. And one of the problems of writing a book about bereavement is that the best and most honest way to write about it is chaotically – which is why I find *A Grief Observed*, the diary C. S. Lewis wrote after his wife's death, the best book on bereavement there is. Imposing some kind of order makes the sufferer – the reader – feel in some kind of control: but is it true? Not really. If there is a major flaw in this book it is that, simply because it is a book, I've been forced to categorize the feelings into different chapters, box them up neatly into tidy little rooms.

I also want to question the many guilt-making theories that surround bereavement and the so-called 'working through' of it – theories that give the impression that if you don't cry and reach rock bottom, then grief will hang around you for ever, like some kind of poison, possibly popping up in the form of dangerous illness, depression or unhealthy behaviour later on. These models are of much more comfort and relief to the people surrounding the bereaved person, who may often seem completely irrational, than to the bereaved person himself, who may wish desperately that he could get from A to B via a convenient swimming pool of tears, but who may find himself, irritatingly, travelling along painful and terrifying viaducts instead. And why not? This is his way, and if bereavement chooses to attack him without allowing him to shed a tear, through the route of crippling headaches or breathlessness, or numbness, or whatever, then that's its own sweet way.

Dr Colin Murray Parkes was one of the first psychiatrists to study bereavement properly in the 1970s. After much research, he was the first to identify these so-called 'stages' of grieving. His model has been as constructive as it has been destructive – constructive in that it has identified a variety of feelings that bereaved people now realize are normal; destructive in that however much Dr Parkes has been at pains to reassure his public that these stages do not have to be experienced one after another, neatly, or last for a fixed period, and that they may overlap, his research is constantly misinterpreted as stages set in stone.

His stages are as follows: 'Numbness, the first stage, gives way to pining and pining to disorganization and despair, and it is only after the stage of disorganization that recovery occurs.'

But does 'recovery' ever really occur? Recovery implies that after a certain time you return to your natural state, but nothing, after a big bereavement, can ever be the same again. Recovery of what? Does recovery mean being able to go back to work? Even if it does, you will not be the same person as you were beforehand, that's for sure.

Other psychiatrists have defined the stages as denial, bargaining, anger, depression and acceptance, and others as shock, disbelief, anger, guilt, depression – and finally resolution. Others have listed numbness punctuated by anger or distress, followed by yearning or searching for the lost figure, which can last for years, followed by a phase of reorganization and despair, with feelings of hopelessness, ending up with a greater or lesser degree of reorganization, and finding a new personal identity.

But we each respond to bereavement individually: one perhaps wanting to keep grief private, one wanting to shout it from the rooftops, one finding physical human contact and loads of hugs and kisses a comfort, others shrinking away and hiding themselves like wounded animals in dark holes. Some may just want to go out and get pissed, others want to repress it all completely. There really is no right or wrong way, and yet still there lurks that counsellor's dream – grief, pain and anger followed by resolution and then, my pet bugbear that usually sneaks in somewhere, enrichment. Maybe you don't get enriched; maybe you do. Or maybe after a bereavement you feel pretty gloomy for ever. This is the thing about bereavement – you can never tell how it will turn out, and any book or counsellor that tells you otherwise is lying.

There is a marvellous description of how dictatorial bereavement counsellors can be in Michael Tolkin's black comedy *Among the Dead*. The wife of the hero, Frank, has just died in an aeroplane crash, and the bereavement counsellor explains the 'process' that lies ahead for him:

'There are a few stages of grief, and I wanted to share them with you, to help you get through them, so you won't feel so alone. The first is denial, which is what you're going through now. And with that, you'll feel alone. That's the isolation stage. Then comes anger, and that's a hard one. After that, well, you'll feel pretty low. The experts like to call that the depression phase; I'd prefer to call it the period of sadness. And then, finally, after the storm, you'll make peace with it. And that's acceptance.'

When Frank's emotions understandably refuse to follow the set pattern, Geoffrey, the bereavement counsellor, tries to put Frank right.

'You know,' said Geoffrey, 'I have to say you seem a little ahead of yourself.'

'How so?' asked Frank.

'I think you've raced a little too quickly from anger into depression. Maybe you need to go back to denial for a bit. After the period where you tell yourself it isn't true, you get really mad. I think you need to be really mad at the airline, at God, at everything.'

'Maybe,' said Frank. He thought this might be true and, thinking back, could not recall any real anger yet. So perhaps he was still denying.

It is this idea that Frank could actually *do* anything about his feelings that is so particularly pernicious. Because my own instinctive feeling is that *you do not work through bereavement. It works through you.*

It is the passivity that's involved in bereavement, the feeling that something terrible is being done to you – which it is – that is the most frightening. And yet bereavement experts keep telling us what to do. For instance, Carol Staudacher claims, in *Beyond Grief*, that you cannot get through grief unless you experience it fully. 'If you hide it, deny it, or dull it, it will only be prolonged. Your emotional pain must be lived through in order for it to be lessened, and gradually eliminated,' she writes, Führer-like in her strictures.

But there are no 'musts' about grieving or bereavement. There is no way that grieving can ever be 'eliminated'! Like many writers on bereavement, Carol Staudacher is on the one hand adamant that you must grieve as you want, that you don't have to go through stages, but she is very happy suddenly to point a bony finger at the reader and utter dire warnings. 'In order to fully realize a death, it is imperative for you to see some evidence of it,' she writes. 'Working though grief and towards an acceptance of what's happened is not easy, but it's essential if the bereaved person is to recover and go on leading a meaningful life.' One fact, she says, remains true for everyone. '*You must not walk around the perimeter of loss.* Instead you must go through the centre, grief's very core, in order to continue your own life in a meaningful way.'

These kinds of statements are neither true nor helpful. Even accepting her circle-shaped metaphor for bereavement, surely some people might be able to walk around and around on the perimeter until, like a circular saw, the centre eventually drops out. Some people might prance around it, some stay sitting quietly just staring at it. They might all experience bereavement. Most, however, would disagree that loss is necessarily something that has a perimeter. The very idea seems to suggest that loss has a shape. Yet what is so very dreadful about bereavement and loss is that the feelings have no shape, no anything. I am tempted to write, Buddhist-style, that loss just 'is'. But even that isn't true. The weird thing about feelings of bereavement is that they can come and go. It is – and it isn't. One day you'll be handing over the money in the supermarket queue feeling perfectly fine, and thinking about supper, and the next minute your knees buckle and you're in floods of tears, overwhelmed by waves of anger, or paralysed by a feeling of nothingness. Bereavement isn't even there all the time. Or, to get even more slippery, for some people it is, for some people it isn't.

Along with the ideas that bereavement has a shape, is a series of stages, or can be 'worked through', there is another popular model, that bereavement is a journey. Like the stages idea, this is extremely useful – but only for those for whom bereavement *is* a journey. Unfortunately for most of us it is not nearly so simple. Some of us find that bereavement is a merry-go-round; others see it as a full-stop; others as a black hole. Lawrence Whistler experienced his feelings after his wife died as some kind of freak storm. In *The Initials in the Heart* he wrote:

> Thus I entered the hemisphere of loss, which has not a weather of its own but a whole new climate of weathers flowing forward without end. They came over me by day and night, in flying fogs and lights of anguish, gratitude, unbearable or assuaging recollection.

Bereavement can also be seen as a disease – but more like malaria than flu, endlessly popping up at odd times and striking its victim down, violent and sweaty, into the foreseeable future. Or is it like a wound? As Elizabeth Jennings wrote:

> Time does not heal,
> It makes a half-stitched scar
> That can be broken and you feel
> Grief as total as in its first hour.

When I had written an article about my father's death someone wrote to me saying: 'I went through it a year ago.' Then she added: 'That past tense doesn't feel right.'

C. S. Lewis felt that bereavement was like an ever-changing and ever-repeating landscape:

> Sorrow however turns out to be not a state but a process. It needs not a map but a history and if I don't stop writing that history at some quite arbitrary point, there's no reason why I should ever stop. There is something new to be chronicled every day. Grief is like a long valley, a winding valley where any bend may reveal a totally new landscape ... not every bend does. Sometimes the surprise is the

opposite one; you are presented with exactly the same sort of country you thought you had left behind miles ago. That is when you wonder whether the valley is a circular trench. But it isn't. There are partial recurrences, but the sequence doesn't repeat . . .

One keeps on emerging from a phase, but it always recurs. Round and round. Everything repeats. Am I going in circles, or dare I hope I am on a spiral? But if a spiral, am I going up or down it? How often will the vast emptiness astonish me like a complete novelty and make me say, 'I never realized my loss till this moment?' The same leg is cut off time after time. The first plunge of the knife into the flesh is felt again and again. They say 'The coward dies many times'; so does the beloved. Didn't the eagle find a fresh liver to tear in Prometheus every time it dined?

Others, however, may see grief as something outside themselves, like a fire, which has to run its course. The flames burn and crackle, and all the victim can do is wait, for weeks, months, even years, until they gutter out. And even then there are always faint embers left which are quite capable of flaring up, as hot as yesterday.

Some find that they can keep bereavement at bay by staying busy. This is a perfectly normal way of coping which works well for some – but if you keep bereavement away by constant action, you may pay for it later. The action may turn out to be an avoidance technique, like putting a finger on the pause button on the bereavement video. When you stop doing whatever you were doing – going to parties, helping others, seeing movies – you still return home to a film which hasn't moved on since you stopped watching it. You can wish and wish you could fast-forward to the end, but you can't.

One widow I talked to did not identify with journeys, videos or fires. She simply likened her tears to a barrel of salt water. They had to be let off in bursts until they were all shed. If she didn't cry, she felt, she would have to carry this barrel around like a burden for the rest of her life. A good image for her – and yet I have met other people who have got over a bereavement without crying. Perhaps, if you expose the tears in a barrel to the sun for long enough, they will, eventually, evaporate.

What is bereavement, then? A series of stages, a process, a journey? None of those images feels right, since they imply a beginning and an end. And while it's comforting to feel that bereavement has an end, I'm not convinced it's true.

The only single truth about bereavement that I can come up with is that it is something that has to be endured alone. True, people on the sidelines can give encouraging waves; other travellers might be able to help over rocky patches; but though our emotional experiences may be similar, none of them are ever the same. Seeing bereavement through the 'journey' metaphor, for instance, some of us may get trapped in dark caves for months; others may scamper through, but find themselves rooted to the spot in what seems like a directionless desert. Some may find that what seemed like a journey has no real ending. The trail simply fizzles out eventually. But even when it has apparently disappeared, years later you can stumble and, looking down, note, with horror, that your footsteps are treading again that dreadful path.

How long does it last? For ever, I would say. But the actual period when you feel utterly screwed up could be anything from six months to six years. Some people feel nothing. Some people never recover. In the Bible, grieving periods have been defined as lasting one or two days (in Ecclesiastes); in Judaic times the third day marked the end of weeping; Joseph was recommended to mourn seven days for Jacob; and in Deuteronomy a reasonable mourning time was thought to be thirty days. Today we're more indulgent with our feelings. It is commonly thought that few people can get over a close bereavement in under a year, if 'get over' is the right phrase to use; one researcher showed that many widows take three or four years to reach stability, whatever stability may mean. Once bereaved, can you ever know stability?

I have been accused more than once of tackling this subject

'too soon' after my father's death. It is now two years since he died. But what does 'too soon' mean? The phrase implies that there is a right time for tackling such a subject, a moment when everything settles down. But if there were a moment when everything settled down again, it would mean that we had forgotten the only thing that bereavement teaches us – that everything is transitory, that nothing can be trusted. And should you trust anything again? No. Surely you should treasure – no, that's not the right word, nothing about bereavement should be treasured, it is so easy to fall into grief-speak – shouldn't you hang on to the reality that everything is unstable rather than fall under the illusion that anything can be trusted to last for longer than just the now?

I hope this is a book that tells the truth about bereavement. It isn't intended to be particularly comforting, because in the face of the pain of bereavement, comfort is only a tiny plaster compared to a gaping wound. And it drops off long before the wound has healed. But telling bereavement how it is, or how it has been for a variety of different people, can throw some light into the darkness. The light may not necessarily show up any pleasant things, but a book on bereavement that doesn't tell you honestly what's what is only a panacea.

When I spoke to a counsellor who had written a book about loss, we touched on the triteness of the idea that anyone would ever 'get over' bereavement. Even the phrase 'come to terms' with a loss seemed unacceptable. I thought that 'living with it' was about the most you could ask for. She suggested that bereavement can be 'assimilated' into people's lives. Then we both agreed that feelings of bereavement never go away. She laughed. 'You're right,' she said. 'But of course, in my book *I couldn't say that*. It's not what people want to hear.' But if she couldn't say it, I'll say it instead. I think people do want to hear the truth. For comfort, have a drink and ring a friend. But there is deeper refreshment to be had: the discovery that other people share confused and often somewhat socially unacceptable feelings as they try, often unsuccessfully, to cope with bereavement.

I've always found books that 'ask more questions than they answer' irritating, on the grounds that if the author had done his homework he would have come up with some clues. Not good enough, is usually my response. But on the subject of bereavement it is the books that *do* come up with answers and advice that irritate me, because when you get to death and bereavement, answers to any questions are inevitably going to be of the glib variety. 'All in the end is harvest.' 'And every winter turned to spring . . .' 'There is an end to grief . . .' 'Death . . . is not an ending but a withdrawal.'

Maybe. Maybe not. I'm not saying, because I don't know. But I do hope that in these pages you will find reassurance that even in your craziest, most evil, most charmless, most miserable, most blanked-off moments, you are not alone. That is, no more, no less, the sum total of what I can offer. But to feel a little less alone at a time when your loneliness is probably acute – well, that is something.

1. Shock and the Physical Effects

The long-drawn-out horror of the previous weeks had produced in me a kind of inert anaesthesia; it was as if I had been so battered and beaten that I was like some hunted animal which, exhausted, can only instinctively drag itself into a hole or lair. (Leonard Woolf after Virginia Woolf's suicide)

What emotion do we most associate with bereavement? Grief. But grief is the primary emotion associated with bereavement only because it is the easiest for society to deal with. The bereaved person hurts; he cries. Someone puts their arm round him, provides a Kleenex, and tells him everything's all right – or tells him to pull himself together or tells him to cry it out or tells him he understands. Everyone, sympathetic and unsympathetic alike, can provide some kind of response to grief. End of story.

The feelings that are much more difficult to deal with are the more private ones – like guilt, feelings of going mad, vivid nightmares, shock; and the socially unacceptable ones – like hatred, anger, joy and hallucinating. The multitude of weird and peculiar feelings is not only terrifying and oppressive for those who experience them first-hand, but also frightening for those who witness their friends experiencing them. It's quite natural to find that most people are far less uncomfortable with the idea that their friends are feeling suicidal after the death of someone close – a ghastly but understandable reaction – than that they are in the grips of wild dreams of blood-stained devils, that they suffer electric shooting pains in their bodies, that they spy their loved one round every corner, that they smell strange smells or feel they are emotional zombies.

Yet these are not only completely natural feelings but much more common than the traditional ones of crying and sadness. And though bereavement counsellors constantly advise crying, many people can't. Tears, longing, sadness – these are the quick short cuts to getting over bereavement. Shoot out of bereavement the way the crow flies; cry your eyes out. Then wipe them. But not everyone can use that salty hotline to the dubious promise of recovery. We cry, yes, but we're constantly side-tracked by these other, less acceptable feelings. And the first uncomfortable side-turning from the roundabout of bereavement that most people are shunted down is the one signposted 'shock'.

Despite what I've said about stages, this is the emotion – or perhaps state would be a better word – that comes first. (It can also come later as well, springing out at us when we're not looking, years after the event. But it pretty much always comes first as well.) True, in books and movies, most people's first reaction on hearing that someone has died is to burst into tears, but, as anyone who has been through a bereavement knows, these are almost always tears of shock rather than grief. They are the tears you might shed after a dreadful road accident, or even a loud explosion, no more than a release of emotion without any particular feeling behind it. But a far more common reaction to bereavement is one of white-faced disbelief, a light-headed sense of unreality, a stunned feeling as though you had been hit over the head with a hammer. It doesn't matter whether you have been prepared for death or not. Death is always an extraordinary surprise. However much we know rationally that all living things die in the end, we are always struck by astonishment when they go.

A middle-aged woman hears that her father, aged a hundred and one, has died. Result? Despite the fact that he was incredibly old and it was really time for him to die, his death is still a shock.

A man suffers from HIV and goes on to develop full-blown AIDS. He and his friends know he will probably live no longer than six months. They see him getting thinner and weaker. But when he dies, they are stunned.

The vet tells a family that their cat has leukaemia and they make a date for him to be put to sleep. But when the day comes, even though they have made the appointment and signed his death warrant, they are horrified and confused to get back home and find the cat's furry body no longer entwining itself round their legs for his evening meal.

'It can't be true!' That's our instinctive reaction to the news of a death. And because we find it so difficult to take in, our bodies immediately go into protective mode. 'When my father died all the members of my family felt as if we had been in a car crash,' said one woman. 'We felt cold and shivery; then our faces burned. I felt light-headed as if I were suspended, floating above everything like a hot-air balloon; that was when I didn't feel my head was filled with molten lead or blood-soaked cotton-wool and buried six feet underground.'

Sometimes people can feel so tense that all their muscles seem to lock, making it difficult to speak. 'I kept stumbling over my sentences; my mouth and jaw didn't seem to work properly,' said one girl after a bereavement.

The shock may manifest itself in symptoms like hammering in the head, knees like jelly and a terrible feeling of unreality. 'It was like me watching them watching me,' said a fifteen-year-old girl whose mother had died. 'I felt like a depersonalized machine.' One friend confided the extraordinary feeling of detachment she had. 'I was by my father's bedside, crying,' she said. 'But all the time I was thinking how good I must look, what a bereaved daughter I must appear to other people. I felt like the bereaved daughter, an actress playing the part, the movie director and the sympathetic audience all at the same time. It was weird.'

What are the symptoms of shock? There are almost too many to mention. Some people experience a curious sensation of feeling burning hot and freezing cold at the same time, often accompanied by utter exhaustion, as if the body is simply unable to cope with the new stresses wrought on it. For months it can be surprisingly difficult to achieve even the simplest task. Just going to the shops may be an enormous effort. 'I would fall asleep for hours in the afternoons, and then go to bed at nine. Then I'd wake up in the night, my heart pounding. I'd wake with a splitting headache, and then these agonizing symptoms might be followed by a strange period of rather sinister calm, as if the body had provided its own tranquillizer to deal with a situation too difficult to handle; it was a rather creepy, serene, high,' said one woman after her husband had died.

'I remember how bruised, physically, I felt, as if I had run full speed into an iron door,' wrote a widower in his diary. 'I remember how impossible I felt it was to drive the car. I walked with my legs wide apart, as though at sea, and couldn't hold up my head.'

Numbness is also common, often causing unnecessary guilt in those who suffer from it, who think that their body's shocked reaction is some gauge of how they felt about the person who has died. It doesn't occur to them that often they feel so very much that, initially, their poor bodies just can't cope with the feelings all at once. As Dr Tony Lake has written: 'The body has a safety mechanism [numbness] that protects us from the tidal wave of emotion that might otherwise push our heart rate and blood pressure up to a physically dangerous level.' Unfortunately, though the numbness can linger for years, in most cases the feelings will follow soon after. Other research showed 'no evidence that [numbness] is an unhealthy reaction. Blocking of sensation as a defence against what would otherwise be overwhelming pain would seem to be extremely normal.'

Lawrence Whistler, writing of his wife's death in *The Initials in the Heart*, said: 'Tears were suddenly replaced by an emotionless and waterlogged calm.'

You may forget things completely, you may feel totally cut off, you may be unable to taste your food, hear properly or even see as well as you used to. You may become surprisingly clumsy, finding plates falling from your hands, and suffering minor car accidents. All the senses may appear simply to have packed up and said 'enough is enough'. Helen Osborne, the widow of John, said when interviewed in the *Daily Mail* by Lynda Lee-Potter:

I'm very strongly aware that I'm not really taking in the fact that he's died. I can't look at a book, I can't concentrate. I don't want to cook, I don't want to eat. Of course I know it's happened but I can't get to grips with it and I can never get warm. I've got so many layers on but I'm always cold.

Sometimes these feelings of shock can appear quite a while after the event. In *Death Plus Ten Years*, Roger Cooper, the businessman kept hostage for years in Iran, wrote:

I am convinced that hundreds, perhaps thousands, of cases of Post Traumatic Stress Disorder go undiagnosed every year. One does not have to have been in combat, gaol or a towering inferno to suffer from this disease: a bitter divorce, a bereavement or even witnessing an accident can trigger it off. It is all the more insidious because of the delayed reactions: the key element in its rather cumbersome title is the word 'Post'. It does not strike until the traumatic event is over and nature has lowered her guard.

Roger Cooper's symptoms manifested themselves in an inability to face driving, or train transport, difficulty with minor tasks like cooking and household jobs, panic attacks, hating unnecessary noise, bad sleeping, nightmares, exhaustion and memory loss, particularly short-term. Three times he started to run water into a wash basin and was distracted by a phone call, flooding his own flat or other people's. Pans burned regularly and pressure-cooker safety valves peppered the ceiling.

I was struck by something of the same kind. Having signed the contract to write this book, and told the publishers how brilliant I was at delivering copy on time, I did all the research and then promptly 'forgot' all about it. I had a vague idea that the manuscript was due in some time, but the subject was something that part of me simply did not want to tackle. My brain shut down. 'No,' it said, for the first time in its efficient life. Even after I started writing the book, the process was dogged by problems with files becoming corrupt and lost, and by tremendous feelings of physical resistance to tackling it, such as headaches, sickness or exhaustion. In the very last stages I managed, rather symbolically, to blow first the memory from my word processor, and then its 'logic board' – apt metaphors at a time when I wished I *could* erase the memory of my loss, and certainly felt that reason and logic had blown away in the explosion of my father's death.

And all this two years on from the moment when I wrote in my diary after my father's death:

> I am writing this at 3.15 in the morning, unable to sleep because of the aches and shooting pains in my legs. I wonder if I should see the doc. I find it quite difficult getting up and down stairs, not that difficult but I am certainly very much aware of each stiff step. Don't like the shooting pains at all. It is quite peaceful now, sort of all cried out, the London night sounds outside.

Aching, and a general feeling of pain in the body, is another very common but somewhat overlooked symptom of grief. If you're anxious or stressed, your muscles tense up, and if they tense up for long enough, as with a bereavement, they can become extremely painful, aching even when you seem to be relaxed. The pain particularly affects the shoulders, the back of the neck and the jaw. 'After my mother died I found it difficult to get up in the morning because my limbs felt crippled with arthritis. My mother did in fact have arthritis,' wrote one woman. It's worth remembering that exercise and swimming, however little you feel like it, can help the physical symptoms, even though they can't ease the emotional ones.

It is not at all uncommon for the people left behind to experience belated 'sympathy' pains with the dead person. A widower friend, whose wife had died of a heart attack, kept telling me how his chest hurt and how frightened he was of having a stroke. Another widow went to the doctor with a piercing pain in her leg – a symptom of the thrombosis from which her husband had died. One woman lost her voice for ten days after her husband's death – he had become unable to speak after a stroke.

There is a common view that the aches experienced in the body are repressed emotions; if only we could let out our feelings and tears we wouldn't suffer. 'Sorrow that has no vent for tears makes other organs weep' is quite a prevalent view, and there is even a theory that arthritis is, in fact, 'crystallized tears'. But pain is pain, whether it is suffered by the body or by the mind; and sometimes the body can bear pain that the mind cannot. Certainly people go to the doctor much more frequently after they have suffered a death in the family. According to research carried out by John Donohue, a clinical psychologist working in Dublin, widows visited doctors six times more than women whose partners were alive; he also claimed that 10 per cent of patients in general hospitals were there because of grief.

It does appear that, since chronic grief and bereavement can affect the immune system, the ailments suffered by bereaved people are not all psychosomatic by any means. The list of symptoms that the bereaved take to the doctor is huge: according to Dr Colin Murray Parkes, the reasons why they visit include nervousness, depression, fears of nervous breakdown, feelings of panic, persistent fears, nightmares, insomnia, trembling, loss of appetite (or, in a few cases, excessive appetite), loss of weight, reduced working capacity and fatigue.

Other symptoms observed by researchers have included headache, fainting spells, 'peculiar thoughts', blurred vision, skin rashes, excessive sweating, indigestion, difficulty in swallowing, vomiting, heavy menstrual periods, palpitations, chest pains, frequent infections and general aching. More? OK. Lump in the pit of the stomach, belching and heartburn, loss of sex-drive (or sometimes an unwelcome increase in sex-drive), muscular pain, constipation. And if that's not enough, add painful heart, no appetite, feet like lead, physical exhaustion, breathlessness ... (no wonder bereaved people are much more likely to visit the doctor than before) ... ringing in ears, digestive problems, nausea, dizziness, constriction in the throat, muscular pain, impeded concentration, poor memory, damp hands, dry mouth, trembling, various gastro-intestinal symptoms, oversensitivity to noise, depersonalization, weakness in muscles, weight loss, amnesia, shaking, absent-mindedness, confusion, drinking, over-spending, over-eating. On top of that, Dr Murray Parkes observed in his study on widows, *Bereavement*, that 'around two thirds of the London widows had a sense of time passing very quickly', describing themselves as 'jumpy, on edge and irritable'. Certainly many bereaved people experience a feeling of 'ants in the pants', always having to be on the go but unable to settle to anything in particular.

Six months after the Labour leader John Smith died, his widow, Elizabeth, was quoted as saying that she'd wake in the morning with thoughts all over the place. Just after he had died and she was on the flight home from London, she went into shock, becoming so freezing cold she had to be wrapped in blankets. 'But after that I became shrouded in this cold calm that enabled me to cope with everything.' Now, she said, that seemed to be wearing off. A couple of months later she looked forward to meeting people but she couldn't take company for longer than an hour. She couldn't concentrate on anything when she was on her own, either, so she didn't have the pleasure of being able to escape into a book or even a TV programme.

Another very common, and peculiar, physical symptom of bereavement is that of unfocused yearning and longing. After the death of anyone close, people are often driven into the streets, looking vaguely for 'something'. They're not really aware of what it is they're looking for, but they may be compelled to roam the town, endlessly window-shopping, restlessly pacing the streets as if hunting. The bereaved will often go for long walks, not really aware of what they're looking for, just knowing that they have to be out, pacing. It is as if some old animal instinct takes over; despite the intellectual knowledge that someone is dead, the muscles seem to respond to some age-old message, and demand to be used in walking, hunting, searching . . .

Sometimes people 'find' what they might be 'looking for'. In the same way that people can occasionally sense a limb even when it has been amputated, bereaved people often 'feel' the sensation of the people who have died. They may sense their comforting presence in a room; or they may actually 'see' them. A GP in Wales revealed that about one in eight of bereaved patients had hallucinations of hearing the dead speak, seeing the deceased or hearing their footsteps.

This 'seeing' is something that usually comes quite soon after a bereavement. We walk down the street – and lo and behold, there is the dead person, alive after all, waiting for a bus. But when we rush up to them, it's all an illusion. I remember 'seeing' my father in church and wondering what on earth he, an agnostic, was doing kneeling in front of me. It is extremely difficult to explain these sightings to other people without being thought completely crazy.

'Sometimes I see someone from the back who looks like her and I think: Maybe she's alive and this is all just a cruel joke. I think maybe she's had amnesia and she doesn't know who she is and I'll go and tell her,' said one son about his dead mother. One woman, after her son's death in a forest, was so aware of his presence there that she actually bought packets of chocolate digestive biscuits – a favourite of his – and went up to the forest to throw them around for him.

Dreams are another characteristic of the physical feelings experienced during early bereavement. Why do I include dreams as 'physical' when they are so obviously imaginary? Because the dreams that people can have following a bereavement are so real and clear that often they feel more poignantly 'real' than the real reality outside which has often, through shock, become a fog. Indeed, bereaved people often dread going to bed because they know their nights will be haunted by hair-raising night-time dramas. Either they will be dreams in which the person lost is actually still alive, and the dreamers will wake, distraught, to find it not true; or they may be dreams about death and destruction. I remember that the most frightening dream I had about my mother was that she was still alive. Since her death was, to me, an enormous relief, I would wake with my heart pounding with fear that my life would once again be burdened with anxiety.

Certainly dreams that dead people are alive, repeated again and again, and constantly shattered when you wake up, may at least serve to ram home the reality of the situation. The fact of death is extremely difficult to absorb. The news that a mother or daughter has died delivered just once, from a nurse, is not good enough. One man was reported to have been with his mother in the morning in hospital when she died, and to have then popped back in the evening 'to bring her some fruit'. Usually the fact of death has to be repeated and repeated – and often the bereaved do this themselves, by endlessly telling people about their loss, and discussing it, to ram the point home. Dreams perform the same function, reminding one again and again of the fact, with the cruel contrast between the dream and reality, that no, the person is in fact dead.

'My sleeping mind was doing the same jumping back in time as my waking mind had that first night she died. I would really be believing that Edie wasn't dead, that we still had a chance, that it wasn't too late,' wrote a mother whose daughter died of anorexia.

> I had long dream talks with her, and we did things together, and sometimes they were so good and she'd be so like her old self that I'd wake up feeling good, like you do after a happy communication with someone. But sometimes they were nightmares – ghoulish monsters, dripping decay; Edie sobbing in the dark, haunted towers and all sorts of horrors.

And then there are those dreams 'where nothing terrible occurs – nothing that would sound even remarkable if you told it at breakfast-time – but the atmosphere, the taste, of the whole thing is deadly'.

Blake Morrison, in *And When Did You Last See Your Father?*, wrote about his terrifying dreams after his father's death.

Dreams? I don't dream of him. I dream of the vast ribcage of a bison lying on the sheet of the desert and being picked clean by vultures. I dream of blistered skin and crumbling parchment and a cyclone of paper bits, a lost mantelpiece blowing about the sky. But I don't dream of him.

Another physical symptom of bereavement can be a deadly euphoria – a feeling of which, naturally, many people feel ashamed. It's not to say that people are necessarily celebrating a death, but they do often feel an unusual kind of sweetness and sharpness about life. Everything is enhanced. Doctors put this down, probably rightly, simply to the increase in adrenalin caused by shock, rather than to any kind of spiritual experience, but it can make some people feel almost blessed or enchanted. It's easy to mistake this adrenalin high, of the sort that you get after any big event, from a wedding to a car crash – or even during jogging – for some kind of mystical reality. Oscar Wilde said: 'Where there is sorrow there is holy ground.' And the Bible tells us that those who mourn are 'blessed'. Of course, in the depth of misery you don't feel in the least blessed. You feel abandoned and betrayed; and yet at the same time you may find your vision leaping into strange focus. Everything important is heightened. Everything unimportant drops away. For a few months, at least, experiences are distilled, sharp – and real. Or apparently real. But are you really more in contact with other people, or is it a feeling no more 'real' than something experienced when smoking dope? Edie's mother wrote:

I felt a tremendous empathy with the whole human race, sensed the common fragility and vulnerability. Whether it was the punk kid, or little old lady, or bowler-hatted businessman, we were all the same, all in this together. This was very important and precious ... It is as if, in the hollow pain, while digging around in the apparent ruin of the present, I struck on the edge of something so much bigger than myself and my family, and yet at one with it. It put our grief into perspective alongside the whole human situation. We all share this together; some in this lifetime – especially in the third world – have a most appalling burden to carry. None is exempt; and this common bond can bring an understanding and empathy which is strengthening and supporting.

The adrenalin high turns every bereaved person, whoever they are, into a philosopher, pondering on big issues. Bereavement may be a painful experience and at the time we may long to get back to the normal shuffle of daily life; but when we do return we sometimes look back and realize those poignant moments could be extremely seductive. As one mourner wrote: 'In the beginning I'd break down and cry; my mother would say: "Give it time." Now, three years later, I can drive past my father's old house without really noticing it. And I feel rather sorry in a way – losing that grief.'

The grass in the field where we grieved may have tasted bitter, and maybe the wind blew sharp and cruel over it, but it really looked greener. As Maria Cantacuzino wrote in *Till Break of Day*, about her experiences as a volunteer with HIV sufferers at the London Lighthouse: 'What I regretted most after leaving Lighthouse was no longer being able to inhabit this raw and passionate world which was so much more substantial than the one which existed outside. Life was richer at London Lighthouse because life was rare and therefore a great deal more precious.'

Some people are hit by a horrible kind of high that usually manifests itself in some kind of obsessional activity. Anyone who has been gripped by this knows that it is not a pleasant feeling at all, more like a crazed feeling of manic depression than a spontaneous burst of energy. But many is the widow who has, in the few days after her husband's death, completely redecorated the house from top to bottom. Staying with friends after the death of my father, I was overcome by a compulsion to clean my car. Not obviously surprising, except that this was a filthy old Metro, covered in rust and bruises, it was the middle of a bitter January and it was eleven o'clock at night. However, dressed in two coats, covered by a mackintosh, in gloves covered by rubber gloves, and with the aid of a torch, I went through every process, from T-cut to polish to chrome polish, ending up wild-eyed and crazed, at three in the morning, with a very smeary car and a pounding heart. I did wonder and worry about my friends' reaction. I wouldn't have blamed them if they'd thought: 'What is the matter? Her father's just died, for God's sake! She should be *grieving* and look at her! Washing her horrible old car! She obviously doesn't care very much!' However, my own pay-off was that I felt in control of something at last.

When does the shock go away? When do the physical symptoms lessen? In *Father's Place*, a widow wrote: 'Realization dawns slowly, like blood returning to frozen fingers, causing excruciating pain before feeling tingles jerkily back to normal.'

But does it? Is this not another romantic's view of bereavement, a comforting approach that's just another lie? If only bereavement were that easy. This is how we would like it to be, to follow a pattern. Shock, numbness, physical illness, followed finally by the jolly old tingles that herald a return to normality.

In fact, sometimes the physical feelings never go completely but linger for ever, like the pink stains caused by something running in the washing machine. And even if the shock itself does fade, there are plenty of other snares on which anyone in the bereavement journey can get snagged. Unfortunately the tingles in the fingertips usually herald not the advent of normality, but rather, like the witches' pricking thumbs in *Macbeth*, a premonition of something wicked this way coming. Something like fear or guilt or anger or all kinds of other dark feelings that we would prefer to pretend do not exist. But those come later. First, some practicalities have to be attended to. The undertaker. The funeral. And the whole ritual of bereavement.

2. The Rituals of Bereavement

I went to the funeral yesterday (it was at the Hampstead Parish Church in Church Row). It was quite dignified but, of course, like all funerals, unpleasant (particularly as it was an interment, not a cremation) ... It is so difficult to describe Bertie's mixture between real and intense sorrow and his faint enjoyment of it all. It is not, of course, the happiest of events – on the surface at any rate. What goes on beneath the surface of one's mind is a different matter. (Patrick Hamilton, writing to his brother Bruce about his mother's funeral)

We are not good at domestic rituals in England. Perhaps we were better in the past, when funerals were big, black affairs, when East Enders hired dark, glossy horses to parade from the dead person's home to the cemetery, but now funerals seem to have lost their way, and are generally rather grimy put-together-at-the-last-minute, try-not-to-think-about-it occasions. Indeed, the whole ritual surrounding death often boils down to a handful of condolence letters, possibly a viewing of the body, followed by a funeral attended only by a few close relatives. Nowadays funerals are sometimes advertised with the gloomy exhortation 'No Flowers, Please', as if flowers were an unseemly display of fun or attention-seeking. If the funeral is held in a church, the deceased and his relations and friends will be unlikely ever to have met the presiding vicar; if at a crematorium, as is most common these days, a rented cleric will preside, a man who, as he delivers a short passage, will read our loved one's name in the place marked X, and remember to substitute 'her' for 'him' as appropriate.

There may be a small party afterwards, known as tea. Later there may be a gravestone, or the ashes will be scattered; then possibly a memorial service, for special occasions. And that's about it. Wham bam thank-you mam. The book of the dead is closed. Back to work. Not so long ago, a bereaved person would wear, at least, a black armband, a visual symbol that would command some kind of respect from strangers in the street, even if this consisted only of a lowering of the eyelids, or a halting of a bubbling laugh. But over the last century the custom of wearing armbands, or just the colour black for long periods, has disappeared, possibly because, during two world wars, there were so many people in England who had suffered a bereavement that, society being united in common grief, symbols were not needed.

In other parts of the world garments may still be rent; sometimes special funeral mourners can be hired to wail and lament. But here and now, in the last part of the twentieth century, bereaved families are not expected to rip their trackie bottoms, or lower their minimalist blinds. No, we are expected to 'get over' a death pretty damn snappily. Our grief has a sell-by date on it.

'We don't draw the curtains any more or wear black or raise our hats – if we had any – when a hearse goes by,' said a team member from the Orchard Project, which offers support and help to children and families facing or experiencing loss. 'These rituals might seem trivial but they used to bring that feeling of togetherness. Now death and grief have been pushed underground and people just don't want to know.'

Condolence letters are the first signs of our shaky ritual, though even this habit is dying out with the art of letter-writing itself. And the next step of the ritual is, usually, the undertaker's invitation to see the body.

Whether to see the body or not is an entirely personal affair. Even you will probably be surprised at your reaction, if you do decide to go – or, indeed, not to go – since it's a decision we are offered so rarely. Some people will decide to take the plunge and after seeing, say, a parent laid out looking completely different to how they did in real life, with, perhaps, a strange expression and a completely new hairstyle, may bitterly regret the decision. Certainly anyone who has freaked out in an undertaker's viewing room will know exactly what Jehane Markham meant in the poem she wrote on seeing her father.

It was like a Building Society without the cashiers,
Grey carpet and wide plastic blind hanging in tiers.
A woman opened a glass-panelled door,
'Have you not seen one before?'
I shook my head,
'I'll stay here, if you like, dear,' she said.
The coffin was open, the lid propped against the wall,
I half expected you to rise up with a mad, laughing leer,
But you didn't move at all.
A cheap night-light burned in an alcove above your head.
I felt the terrible stillness of you instead.
There was blackness in your mouth
But worse than this,
your fingers had been forced into a prayer;
a rosary and cross hung upon your chest,
giving you a pious air
which in your life you never possessed.
You wore your best shirt that your daughter, Molly, chose.
It was bad to see you dead and dressed in clothes.

One young man who saw his father laid out said:

I was shocked. His hair had been centrally parted and
slicked down with Brylcreem, and he looked more like an
elderly bank clerk than the rather glamorous, laid-back old
hippie that he was in life. It might have been better to get a
close friend to have gone in first to help the undertaker get
it at least half-way right before getting it totally wrong. I'm
glad my sister didn't see him.

But other people, deciding not to take up the undertaker's
invitation, may regret that they were never brave enough to witness their dead relative. 'I never saw her because I was too frightened,' said one girl about her grandmother. 'I think I found it
much more difficult to accept she had died because at the back of
my mind I keep thinking she didn't really die and I might meet
her in the street, even twenty years later when it's impossible.'

For others, however, the sight of the body brings immense comfort. The experience can be especially important to parents, who often bitterly regret not seeing children who have been, say, badly smashed up in a road accident. Bemused with shock, they may take the advice of well-meaning friends or partners who assure them that it is best to remember the child 'as they were', and it is only later that they realize they'd rather have seen any kind of horror than not have seen the child at all. One woman whose son had killed himself under a train was told the body was so badly mutilated she shouldn't see it – or even look at the police photographs. But a year later she went to the coroner's office and though she found the pictures upsetting they gave her a sense of resignation. She has no regrets.

Some mourners break down and cry, and have to be torn away from the body by relatives. Perhaps they sense that in this dead shell, the loved one is actually 'still there' – and, like a child clinging to its mother's skirt as she whisks out of the front door, realize that to say goodbye to the body is indeed goodbye. Others may feel a great sense of joy when they see their loved one's face finally relaxed – particularly if that face has been, for the past few years, etched with the pain of a prolonged illness. Others come away from the viewing carrying some kind of acceptance of the fact of death. 'I didn't cry a drop until I saw my mother in her coffin,' said one man. 'It was the moment her death really came home to me.'

Finally, there is a very common reaction – a kind of peace that has more to do with what the person visiting the dead body feels to be a new knowledge about death than with grieving for a particular person. 'We could only see her head and shoulders – I imagine the rest had been mangled up by the post-mortem,' said one woman, who took her six-year-old son to see her mother, who had died of cancer.

Her face was white, covered in powder rather like flour. It looked quite unnatural until I realized that that was what it was – unnatural. She was absent. It was as if I'd come into the room looking for my mother and been shown a pile of old clothes in a box and I'd said: 'Oh, no, that's not my mother, those are her clothes, but where is she?' I'd been expecting a sight to haunt me, and I hadn't imagined death to look so ordinary or so 'dead'. It was just harmless dead flesh and bones, like the cast-off skin of an old snake. Something she'd lived in when she was alive. So where was she? 'Somewhere,' I reasoned, in a moment of revelation. The whole trip comforted me, because it made me realize with utter certainty both her absence and her presence.

(I have to say here that there is still a big difference between seeing a dead body at the undertaker's and seeing one untouched at home. 'The worst thing I ever did was to see the body of my friend who had died of AIDS,' said one twenty-five-year-old man. 'He was the colour of pale blueberry and when I kissed his cheek he was freezing with death, only a few hours after he had gone. Since then, I've always felt uncomfortable about the way death is portrayed in films. Bodies dead for days still look pink and healthy. But in real life it's nothing like that. People really do turn into corpses.')

However, seeing a dead body does ram home the message that our minds and our bodies, quite naturally, resist: that the dead person is *dead*. It's one thing to know, intellectually, that someone has died; another to accept it at a deep, unconscious level.

Ramming home the fact of a death is the function of the major ritual after a death – the funeral, society's way of telling us that not only do you know he or she is dead, but yes, everyone else knows it, too. The announcement is to be made publicly, over a coffin, while the bereaved are surrounded by kind friends, all helping them to acknowledge the unacknowledgeable. And even the most restrained of British funerals tell us something. Even if you are not close to the dead person, even if you are simply a stranger who sneaks in to someone else's funeral and

18

stands at the back of the church, you will still be forced to recognize the mystery and horror of death, a moment when you are unable to resist some vague sense of spirituality crawling into a crack in your life. Few are the mourners who don't look at that wooden box and think, at the very least: 'Cripes, one day it's going to be me in there.' Is it surprising, therefore, that a funeral can be such a traumatic event for the bereaved? Not only does the event emphasize that someone has gone, it also emphasizes the inescapable fact of our own mortality. Two body-blows in one day. And other realizations may be heaped on by the spadeful during this short ceremony. In view of the myriad of emotional experiences the funeral encompasses, it is fairly astonishing, indeed, that the whole service itself usually takes no longer than three-quarters of an hour.

For instance, for some the funeral can represent the existence of the person as well as the death. 'It was so hard coming home to the children,' said one mother whose baby had been stillborn. 'The oldest two were very upset and could not understand why their baby had died. I had brought a special outfit to bring him home from hospital in, so he was dressed in that, and wrapped in the shawl I had made for my youngest son. The funeral was just a small service at the graveside. To have somewhere to go with flowers is a comfort to us both.'

Funerals also offer a sense of power and purpose to those left behind, by giving them something constructive to do. Poring over virtually unread bibles searching for suitable quotes, telephoning vicars asking about hymns, discussing tunes with organists, making out the guest list, and wondering whether to ask an aunt loathed by the deceased but who would be mortally hurt not to be invited, discussing with undertakers which size of coffin to buy – all these may be grisly but also therapeutic tasks. One of the disadvantages of the fashion of organizing and paying for your funeral in advance is that these arrangements remove all power from the people left behind. It may be painful to have to decide whether to have the cedarwood or the oak coffin and whether it should have brass handles or not, but it gives the bereaved something to focus on, and feeds survivors' fantasies that they are doing something for the dead person, even though in reality they are only doing something for themselves. Again, this feeling of giving can be an extremely healing process.

'We really pulled together for the funeral,' said one man when his sister died.

> We were all given a task to do by Mum. One hoovered the living-room, another made the sandwiches – some smoked salmon and some cheese and chutney because Mum loved those – another acted as usher at the church, I read a lesson and tipped the vicar, my brother tipped the gravedigger, my aunt designed the map so guests could find their way . . . It was great. We were all busy. Old scores were forgotten and we really pulled together. She would have loved that, I know.

Since the reverse of the coin of loss – longing for something – is not gain, but rather the feeling of being longed for, or needed, it follows that everyone needs to feel needed after a bereavement, even if their tasks are completely manufactured. DIY funerals are increasingly popular, giving enormous satisfaction to some bereaved people, who can find great fulfilment in purchasing a cardboard or papier-mâché coffin, perhaps getting it painted by relatives, driving the car containing the coffin to a crematorium themselves, and generally making the whole funeral a thoroughly family affair. It also gives every family member a chance, after death, to put right the personal debts they feel to the dead person. You may feel that you didn't visit the dead person enough when they were ill – but by God, you'll make damned sure that the coffin looks beautiful and the service is perfect, to make up for the areas in which you failed them before. It also gives the family a chance to build something in a world that has been destroyed. Many is the bereaved person who has found streaks of creativity in times of loss – through poetry, letters, diaries, paintings. It is as if they have to create to make up the balance lost through the death of someone close.

For others, the funeral symbolizes stability in an unstable world. 'It sounds bad to say you enjoyed a funeral but I did,' said one widow.

After Brian died, my life had been in chaos until that moment. I couldn't do a thing. I was crying all the time. My doctor gave me pills. I thought I couldn't go to the funeral – my son arranged it all. And then when I got there it was, well, beautiful. I haven't been to church since I was seven, my grandmother used to take me, but it felt as if I was coming home. The smell of it, the light through the windows, the sound of the organ music, the whole ceremony, well, it was all a sign that everything was going to be all right eventually. Everything was still here, in a way. It was sort of everything had gone wrong, I felt completely at sea, and yet inside this church there was this service going on, and it would always go on when anyone died, and suddenly I felt that Brian's death was part of something bigger.

The funeral can also jerk people out of shock and into grief, acting as a starting pistol for their emotions. Maria Cantacuzino wrote:

In my experience, when people you don't know very well die, it is easy to have a quick gush of sadness and then get on with your life as before. With Julian, even that gush was repressed because I was surrounded by people who I felt had more right to grieve than I had. The funeral, however, sorted out all these mixed emotions and my sadness suddenly broke through all the barriers which I had unconsciously erected.

While some people find that the funeral heralds an opening of the floodgates, however, others may be embarrassed to find that they can neither feel nor express anything at all – embarrassed particularly because a funeral is one of the few social occasions during which grief is not only acceptable, but as nearly encouraged as any display of strong emotion is in our society. 'I sat through it quite dry-eyed, and I thought everyone must think I was a cold fish,' said one widower. 'But in fact my friends described me as "terribly brave". The reality was that my feelings were blanked off and I wasn't brave at all. They should have seen me after they'd all gone home. I wonder if they'd have called me "brave" then.'

'My brother-in-law had a private funeral for my sister when she died. He didn't ask anyone, and has never mentioned her name again,' said one distraught sister. 'He seems to have blanked off completely, unable to realize how important it was for the rest of us to have some kind of ceremony. We had to organize a private ritual of our own.'

The funeral is the last time that the bereaved will be in the same physical space as the dead person. It is a very graphic 'goodbye', whether the coffin is shunted electronically through velvet curtains, or lowered six feet into the ground. It is at the funeral, too, that so many people experience the terrible paradox: are they present to celebrate a life or mourn its passing? I remember a particularly difficult moment when, at the funeral of three young cousins who had died in a fire, their father announced, at the tea afterwards, that today was one of their birthdays. I couldn't work out what this statement was meant to signify. Did that mean we should cheer and wish the dead child happy birthday? Or did the fact add bitter poignancy to the occasion? And these moments are often metaphors for our own feelings. Should we be celebrating the beginning and end of a wonderful and fulfilling life, or mourning the loss of it? Is grief the only emotion we experience – or are there things about the dead person that we are glad to see the back of? At a funeral one foot is so often on the brake, and another on the accelerator. No wonder feelings of bereavement are so excruciatingly difficult to deal with.

In some societies double burials are carried out. After the body has been buried for some time it's dug up and re-interred.

This is done, apparently, to identify and mark a new relationship with the dead person. The first time the body is buried as a relation; the second time it is buried as an ancestor. There is a great deal of sense in this. The nearest we get to it is when a dead person has many, many friends all over the country. Then the funeral is usually carried out rather hastily, with only a few relations attending, and is followed, sometimes months later, by a much more carefully planned and loving memorial service. The funeral is the time for tears; the memorial a time for celebration. The memorial service, too, can be worked on for much longer by the family, who may have been too dazed to choose much more than a kind of Chinese set meal of a funeral from the church's menu. Crimond? Yup. Love Divine? Yup. John 11: verses 25–6? Yeah, yeah, whatever you say. And some prawn crackers and a pot of jasmine tea while you're at it.

But how should this dead person be remembered? As a human being, warts and all, or, as is far too common, as a saint? Never has there been such an obstacle to getting anywhere near incorporating the death of someone into one's life than the chilling phrase: 'Never speak ill of the dead.' 'It may even happen that death will award a belated certificate of good conduct,' wrote Jean Cocteau. 'Well! we cannot help thinking, this man has just died. He is undeniably dead. So he wasn't just an ordinary man. Perhaps he was a better man than he seemed.' In *When Parents Die*, Rebecca Abrams wrote:

> More than anything I loathed the sanctification of my father, a process that began to take place almost immediately he was dead. I knew him as bad-tempered, difficult, anti-social, allergic to physical exercise. And I knew him also as clever and sensitive and rather fun and mischievous. All of these made up the father I loved. It was terrible to hear him turned into some kind of saint. People said things that simply weren't true. It didn't help me at all, this enshrining in saintly characteristics. It merely increased the sense of unreality, the feeling that nothing was real or sure or

reliable any more. And it increased my sense of profound isolation; the sensation that I was utterly alone with my loss and grief. No one understood how I felt, because no one understood what I had lost.

It is also at funerals and memorial services that small irritations can turn into huge ones. It is when the vicar gets the name of the loved one wrong, or the best friend, who gives the oration, makes a tiny omission or mistake, that the raw skin of the bereaved is pierced as if by red-hot needles. At my own (twice-married) father's funeral, his friend gave the most wonderful address that summed up his best points completely. But this friend failed to mention my mother's name in it at all, as if his life with her – and therefore myself – had never existed.

'The worst moment was when the vicar said of my friend that he loved the arts and the theatre. In fact he loved the arts – the visual arts – but hated the theatre and books,' said one girl whose friend had died. 'The fact that he slipped up so publicly made a mockery of everything else he said. I felt he had been caught out in a lie. I felt very disappointed. And because it was all so public, my angry feelings were compounded.'

Then how should you behave at a funeral? There is no 'should' about it, needless to say, because a funeral is a journey into outer space. You may set off for the church or crematorium imagining that because you will be attending a structured service there will be little opportunity for emotional chaos. But nothing goes according to plan. Those who look forward to being able to collapse with tears often remain tense and dry-eyed; those who think they will keep a stiff upper lip may have to be helped, staggering with grief, from the church. Funerals are rather like ghost trains; you never know when you are going to be slapped in the face with the stringy, slimy hand of grief, or, almost worse, surprised into embarrassing giggles by a leering phosphorescent skull.

But however awkward and fumbling most funerals are, they are usually better than nothing. Worst of all is to be completely uninvolved. It is during a funeral that an ex-wife, ex-parents-in-law, a mistress, the gay lover, never acknowledged by the family, can feel most painfully excluded. 'I had been having an affair with Emily for four years,' said one man.

She was going to leave Jonathon [her husband], who was an absolute shit, when her daughter was eighteen, next year. We were so happy and loved each other so much. But no one knew. I wasn't even a friend of the family. I found out where the funeral was and I hung around the churchyard outside until I could bear it no longer. When I went in, no one noticed me. But I had to leave because I was making so much noise – I was overwhelmed with grief. I sat in the car and watched everyone leave, and I saw Jonathon propped by relatives, and I thought, you bastard. Then I went to a pub and had a cheese sandwich and a pint and sat in the car thinking I was going quite crazy. Eventually I drove back, and went to see my doctor and explained the situation and he gave me tranquillizers and I took some time off work. I still haven't recovered and I don't think I ever will. I never even had a chance to say a proper goodbye. I have nothing of hers to remember her by. We were so careful we never even took photographs of each other. I went to look at her grave recently, but it had written that she was the 'beloved wife of Jonathon' and of course I just turned and came home and never went back. I sometimes wonder whether our time together was actually real and not a figment of my imagination.

The other people who can feel neglected and powerless are children. Even nowadays, children are often left at home during funerals, like dogs. Why should children be excluded from funerals when they're so welcome at christenings and weddings? Not only can their presence be therapeutic for other adults and useful reminders that life, whatever death may do, goes on; not only is it unlikely that very young children will be upset, simply because they have only a vague idea of the concept of death.

But not attending the funeral of someone close can be tremendously damaging for some people in later life. Middle-aged people who were not allowed to attend the funerals of grandparents or even parents, can still feel full of rage and sorrow.

'My father was ill one day and I was sent on holiday for two weeks to friends,' wrote one woman.

When I was returned, my father was gone and I was told that he was with God. Oh well, I thought, he'll be home soon. It took four years for me to fully realize the truth, that he was never coming back, that he was dead. My overwhelming emotion was anger that I had been lied to and not allowed to mourn and share grief with my mother and those closest to him.

True, children might be worried at seeing their mother or father break down and cry, but in the long term it might be better to see a parent express strong feelings and recover than to be excluded from the whole event altogether. Attending the funeral can also help a child make sense of tense or ratty behaviour in his parents in the weeks that follow – behaviour that otherwise might well be a mystery to a child, who could take it personally. Death is a great taboo that holds much fear for all of us; if that taboo can be broken down early on, at least a little, it can help protect the child when he or she may have to face your own death.

After the funeral there is usually some kind of get-together when the mourners go back somewhere for tea or a drink – and there are no set social rules for how this event should be organized. Yet again the bereaved face the old dilemma. Should it be a sad and serious reunion of friends and relations, or a celebration? Tea and sandwiches, or champagne and canapés?

After Roy Castle's celebratory funeral, the late John Osborne wrote, in the *Mail on Sunday*, of his concern about what he felt was forced joyfulness surrounding his death.

Doubtless it is one way of expressing that the whole messy

business of life is over and it is time for a good knees-up with God. But of course it isn't 'over'. Celebration, like protest, is easy. Grief comes harder. Bereavement is not a medical condition and its abiding sorrows will not be dispelled by putting on a happy face. Perhaps this party-time response was the only way his family could cope with that terrible trial which faces each one of us.

What a party does do, however, is comfort the bereaved. Old friends, old relations you hadn't seen for years – they are all there, all as pleased to see you as you are to see them, all as eager to heal old rifts and make new contact. Their presence can be a balm. The dead person has gone – it is a time when you need to count who is left, who is still there on your side. Dreary old relations you might have taken somewhat for granted look warm and sparkling. They may not be soulmates, but at least they are still here. They are alive, they aren't dead, and they love you.

There may be an empty feeling after the memorial or funeral service. But one last ceremony remains: there is a grave to be visited and tended, or even a field where ashes have been scattered. 'When I took your ashes to the Downs it was a solemn moment,' wrote one widower in a diary to his late wife. 'Your face and body, the lovely soft lips and breasts you took such care of, the grey blue eyes and the rather diffident smile, the long delicate fingers exactly, you liked to say, like your father's, all in that grey powdery dust.'

The idea is that these locations serve as a ritualized focus for feelings of bereavement. Every time the spot is visited, the feelings come out. Or that's the plan, at least. It doesn't always work like that.

While my father's gravestone was being made, I worked myself up into a fantastic to-do over its design, beside myself with misery and rage that I had not been privy to the choosing of what kind of stone it would be. I felt utterly lost and abandoned, as if I counted for nothing. It was, I know, nothing personal and simply an oversight; no one, least of all myself, could have predicted how violent my feelings would have been. And while I was as thrilled as if I'd won the World Cup when I had finally manipulated some special little spots to be engraved on it – '*my* spots' – whenever I visit the grave now I am left totally cold. I can stare at it till the cows come home and feel not a drop of grief. Yet one man wrote, after being present at the setting of his father's stone: 'I touched it and it felt warm, as if it were him, alive. That stone meant so much to me. It cost a lot, but it was worth it because to me it means his memory is still alive.' And some visit graves for comfort and communion. 'I go every week to my husband's grave,' said a widow. 'I talk to him, discuss what's happened in the week, and ask his advice. I usually get it, too! Though I'm sure a lot of people think I'm mad, sitting on my own in the graveyard, talking to myself!'

In *Patrimony* Philip Roth described his own feelings when visiting his mother's grave. They turned out to be not ones of reassurance or sadness, simply cold confirmation that yes, she had truly gone.

I find that while visiting a grave one has thoughts that are more or less anybody's thoughts and, leaving aside the matter of eloquence, don't differ much from Hamlet's contemplating the skull of Yorick. There seems little to be thought or said that isn't a variant of 'he hath borne me on his back a thousand times'. At a cemetery you are generally reminded of just how narrow and banal your thinking is on this subject. Oh, you can try talking to the dead if you feel that'll help; you can begin, as I did that morning, by saying, 'Well, Ma . . .' but it's hard not to know – if you even get beyond a first sentence – that you might as well be conversing with the column of vertebrae hanging in the osteopath's office. You can make them promises, catch them up on the news, ask for their understanding, their forgiveness, for their love – or you can take the other, the active approach, you can pull weeds, tidy the gravel, finger the letters carved in the tombstone; you can even get down and place your hands directly above their remains – touching the ground, *their* ground, you can shut your eyes and remember what they were like when they were still with you. But nothing is altered by these recollections, except that the dead seem even more stationed out of reach than they did when you were driving in the car ten minutes earlier. If there's no one in the cemetery to observe you, you can do some pretty crazy things to make the dead seem something other than dead. But even if you succeed and get yourself worked up enough *to feel their presence*, you still walk away without them. What cemeteries prove, at least to people like me, is not that the dead are present but that they are gone. They are gone and, as yet, we aren't. This is fundamental and, however unacceptable, grasped easily enough.

This knowledge is what the rituals are all about. They are to bring home to all of us that we will never see the dead person ever, ever again. Caput. Finito. End of story. And once you accept that, then you either feel a great peace coming over you, or you feel nothing, or you feel overcome with grief and sadness. Or you feel a cold chill running up and down your spine.

Fear.

3. Fear

No one ever told me that grief felt so like fear. I am not afraid, but the sensation is like being afraid. The same fluttering in the stomach, the same restlessness, the yawning. I keep on swallowing.

At other times it feels like being mildly drunk, or concussed. There is a sort of invisible blanket between the world and me. I find it hard to take in what anyone says. Or perhaps, hard to want to take it in. It is so uninteresting. Yet I want the others to be about me. I dread the moments when the house is empty. If only they would talk to one another and not to me . . . (C.S. Lewis, *A Grief Observed*)

Death is a taboo subject. The subject makes us shudder. 'How gloomy!' people exclaim if we bring up the subject. 'Can't we talk of something more cheerful?' Once, when I was discussing suicide in a quiet voice with a dinner guest on a sofa, my conversation was interrupted and hijacked by a man who squeezed himself between us and insisted that we get off what he called 'the dismal topic'. In vain did we assure him that we were fascinated; no, he insisted on telling us instead about so-called 'good news' – how much money he had made on a property deal, a topic we found infinitely more depressing than suicide.

His reaction was the norm, however. We do not talk of death because we are terrified of it. If we say the words: 'When I die . . .' listeners will touch wood, or say: 'Oh, don't say that . . .' or 'You're being very morbid.' No one would ever dream of saying: 'When you die . . .' to anyone. At least, not without adding many clichéd qualifications, crossing their fingers rather obviously, or saying, jokily: 'Well, not that I want you to die, but we all have to go sometime . . .'

Even if an extremely old person remarks on the fact that she is going to die soon, an incontrovertible fact if she is, say, a hundred years old, most people will usually shake their heads and mutter things like: 'No, you've got ages to live yet,' despite all evidence to the contrary. Just speaking about death is seen as tempting fate; speaking about it might, God forbid, actually bring death on.

One of the reasons that wills are usually made in private and not discussed in advance of death is that either the will-maker, however ancient he is, finds it unbearable to consider his death in advance, or, if he wishes to discuss it, he's met with great resistance from his family. 'Oh, come on, it's too depressing, don't let's think about it, what's the matter with you . . . Wills? You shouldn't be thinking about those at your age.'

Why are we frightened of death? We are terrified of the un-known; we are terrified of how we may feel when someone dies – lost, lonely and bereft; we are terrified to think that we may die ourselves. Fear is one of the biggest emotions after bereavement. Who knows, really, what death is actually about? We haven't a clue. We put fear in its place. What did C. S. Lewis mean when he wrote the line, 'I am not afraid, but the sensation is like being afraid'? Surely he felt frightened because he *was* frightened.

Perhaps he was frightened of abandonment. His wife had once said to him: 'Even if we both died at exactly the same moment, as we lie here side by side, it would be just as much a separation as the one you're so afraid of.'

Fear of abandonment is what we fear, separation anxiety – a state that takes us right back to that time when, as babies, we were tiny and vulnerable, and totally dependent on our parents. Loss of someone close must always give us just a whiff of a reminder of what the loss of a parent might have meant to us. It could have meant loss of ourselves. It could have meant extinc-tion before we had ever properly lived.

Death brings close the idea of our own mortality – a frighten-ing thought. Tolstoy conveyed those feelings of panic when he wrote *The Death of Ivan Ilyich*. His colleague, Piotr Ivanovich, had come to view Ivan's body.

The thought of the sufferings of the man he had known so intimately, first as a light-hearted child, then a youngster at school, and later on, when they were grown up, as a partner at whist, suddenly struck Piotr Ivanovich with horror . . . He again saw that brow, and the nose pressing down on the lip, and was overcome with a feeling of dread on his own account.

'Three days and nights of awful suffering and then death . . . Why, it might happen to me, all of a sudden, at any moment,' he thought, and for an instant he was terrified.

When my father died I was terrified, too, and acutely aware of what Proust said: that the living are simply dead people who have not yet taken up their posts.

Some bereaved people find themselves dealing with this fear in a kind of wild, swashbuckling way. They may become reckless, driving the car at breakneck speed, drinking too much, crossing the road without looking, as if, once death has been met, it must be embraced, flirted with, and made friends with. Others become supersensitive. Death seems to stalk every street with his skull-like face and his scythe. He seems to have acquired a passport into our own personal country; he's already visited one famous sight, and what other tourist attractions might he have marked in red now he is here? What other souvenirs would he like to take with him back to his underworld? Who else has he got his beady eye on? At some subconscious level the bereaved often worry that they may have an accident, that they are dying themselves, often having to visit the doctor with the same symptoms of the disease that has killed the loved one. We may become hypochondriacal about our own health – and of those around us.

Bereaved parents suddenly panic when their children drive the car. They may find they cannot bear those close to them to go away. Childishly they fear they may never see them again. After my father died, my son went on a fortnight's holiday to Greece, a long-planned trip. I gave him a lift to the airport (as much from longing to stay as near to him as possible till the very last minute as out of the kindness of my heart), and as he left he gave me a special hug and said: 'Oh Mum, I hate leaving you when you seem so tense and sad.' His kindness made the parting almost worse. Because my father had gone, I felt cut off from the land on one side; when my son went away, it was as if the water had suddenly flowed round and cut me off completely. All exits had been closed and I was completely on my own. I was stranded on a desert island. True, it was only for two weeks, but two weeks is a long time, particularly when I was convinced that the ferry to the Greek island my son was visiting would sink, or that he would be certain to ride a motorbike without hiring a helmet and be instantly killed. Well, of course he would, wouldn't he? Death, I was certain, was shadowing our family's every move.

When a parent dies, younger children can feel terrified that the remaining parent will die, too, leaving them completely alone. In *How It Feels When a Parent Dies*, Jill Krementz quotes two children who were left with only one parent. Jack, an eight-year-old whose father had committed suicide, said:

I don't really talk about my father very much. I talk to my mother once in a while but I usually keep my feelings to myself. I don't want my mother to start crying because if she starts crying she starts coughing and stuff and then I get worried that she'll have to go back to the hospital. She's had kidney stones about four times and when that happens we have to stay with Aunt Bessie or one of our grandmothers. So I worry that her kidney stones are going to get worse and worse and the next thing you know – pop! There she goes, too.

And a nine-year-old girl, whose father had died of cancer, said:

The thing I'm most terrified of right now is that my mother may also die. I've had a few dreams about her, of something happening to her, and whenever I have these kinds of nightmares I wake up crying because I'm so scared. This year my cat died and before that, my grandfather died and so did my mother's best friend. It just seems as though so many people in my family have died, and when someone dies, it's just like taking away a part of me . . .

When people die one after another – as tends to happen when they get old – the people left alive may feel extremely shaky and flaky. Some homosexuals, who have experienced the death of many, many friends cut down by AIDS, may become quite ill and paranoid. Maria Cantacuzino wrote that a very small proportion of the bereaved at London Lighthouse developed 'symptoms of paranoia, believing themselves to be surrounded by evil, either self-inflicted or instigated by some supernatural force'.

It may be only a small proportion who suffer the full-blown craziness, but there can't be a bereaved person anywhere who hasn't experienced a whiff of that terror of the supernatural; who has not perceived, if only in dreams, the corner of death's black garment, even if it is only disappearing swiftly through a crack in a door; who hasn't howled out, in the middle of the night: 'Why me?' as if death had picked them out among thousands of others for special torture.

All change is frightening, and for bereaved partners their fear may be of a very basic kind. They may be terrified, like children, of simply 'being on their own'. This fear is separate from the uncomfortable and upsetting feelings of having a new role and a new place in your social and family jigsaw, a situation which is discussed in a later chapter; this is a more basic, primitive fear associated with survival. Sleeping on your own . . . (Did the burglars read about his funeral? Will they decide that tonight's the night to prey on a lonely widow at home?) Cooking for yourself . . . (I can't do it, I don't understand the oven, will it explode or will I starve to death?) Coming back to an empty house . . . (Will I go mad with no one to talk to? Who am I?) Attempting new and unfamiliar household tasks . . . (Did I fix that plug correctly? Will I be electrocuted? How do I know when the car needs a service? Maybe it will break down tomorrow when I'm on the motorway.) Filling in forms . . . (I'm sure I've forgotten something. I don't think the bank understands what I meant. I'll face financial ruin. I'll be on the streets . . .)

Some people fear going to sleep because of the dreams they experience; some people fear getting out of control with grief and going mad. Even those relieved by someone's death do not escape from fear and the pounding heart. 'When my mother, a paranoid schizophrenic, died, I thought I felt no fear,' said one daughter. 'I felt only relief that she had gone. Until I dreamt that her death was only a manipulative schizoid trick, and that really she was alive all the time. I woke up drenched in terror.'

Like shock, fear doesn't always come right after a death or, necessarily, in great big bursts. Fear can hang about, an unwanted guest in your mind, for years. Some people find they feel most fear when they themselves reach the age that their parents were when they died. A common reaction to suicide is a fear that one might do it oneself, and many relatives of suicides have felt tremendous relief when they pass the age at which the suicide killed himself. 'Until I was forty, when my father died, I didn't know what I was so frightened of,' said a man whose father died of a heart attack.

I was getting more and more anxious, and my fortieth birthday was hellish. Everyone thought I was just being vain, but now I realize that I was terrified of what I thought was my own inevitable death. After my forty-first birthday I felt tremendous peace. To be honest I now realize that I wasn't really living until I was forty. I couldn't ever make any long-term plans. I felt extremely guilty about having children. Only now, twenty-five years after my father's death, can I start living. I have stopped being afraid.

4. Powerlessness and Guilt

> The night of the funeral I dreamed the dream again, the one I'd had since childhood. A forest in autumn, fallen leaves drifting this way and that over the ground, rustling in a thoroughly sinister manner. Nothing else occurs except that there am I, rooted to the spot, the solitary soul in the world who knows that under those leaves, under that ground, lies a body and that one day it will be discovered and I will be revealed as the murderer. (Jill Tweedie, in *Eating Children*, describing her feelings when her father died)

The feelings of helplessness that follow a bereavement can be worse by far than the feelings of grief. Why did that person have to die? In the usual Gothic language of bereavement books, one writer tried to define death as 'the most unfathomable mystery of humankind'. But pinning death down as an unfathomable mystery is to simplify it, to stop the madness. The answer to why someone died is not the slick reply, 'Because death is an unfathomable mystery.' There is no 'because' about it. The answer is simply the cruel, mocking, angry echo back. Why? Why? If only we could find a reason for death, how much easier it would be to deal with.

Not only are there no apparent motives for the murder, as it were, but there are no signposts for life ahead. Those left behind face an uncharted future afloat the perilous seas of powerlessness.

A recently bereaved widower commented despairingly to me, after his wife had died, that he would just have to resign himself to a miserable life waiting to die. And he complained because his neighbours had disagreed. They predicted that life was going to be rosy for him in the future; at last he'd be able to go away on cruises and get chased by glamorous widows. But neither his gloomy prognostications nor the optimistic predictions of his neighbours were necessarily true; the truth – and it's a less easily

digestible truth than either option – is that when you are bereaved you have absolutely *no idea* what lies ahead. The journey is
– what? Where are you going? Are you going anywhere? Is there
in fact a journey awaiting you at all? Perhaps the future consists
of just the same series of ghastly bleak question marks blipping
endlessly on the screen, like signs on a crashed computer. You
might find that as one door closes, as the cliché goes, another
opens, and there's a new and interesting life ahead; equally you
might plunge into depression and find that as one door closes,
all the others lock and bolt themselves shut as well. It all depends on timing, personality, chance, God, higher power, fate,
circumstances . . . But many people prefer to imagine the depressing 'certainty' of a miserable future than face the terrifying
unknown.

Working as an agony aunt and spending quite a lot of my
time trying to help people, I found it impossible to be remotely
interested in other people's problems after my father died. One
day I sat on the office floor looking for a book called *Grief* to
take home, and suddenly found I couldn't get up from my spot
in front of the bookcase. I had no energy, chained down by an
inability to do anything at all. I felt like just sitting there and
waiting for someone to take me away in a sedan chair; or I
thought perhaps if I stayed long enough, the cleaners would
come in the morning, throw me into a black binbag and dispose
of me. It wasn't that I felt unhappy. I was simply stricken with
the most terrible feeling of helplessness.

When faced with powerlessness, the temptation is, naturally,
to 'do something' – which is why the funeral service can have a
healing effect. Only a day after the death of his wife my widower friend, in a manic phase that is also common in bereaved
people, suddenly lurched into wild, energetic action, wondering
if he should get a job as a voluntary worker, whether he should
move, whether he should get a dog. He was desperately grasping
for some control over his shattered life. But the balance of his
mind was completely disturbed and it is small wonder that the
advice of all bereavement counsellors is to make no drastic

changes in one's life until at least a year after the death of a loved one, however strong the temptation to 'do something' may be.

Talking or writing about the death is one way of trying to regain control. Many bereaved people report an urge to express the event in words – publishers are inundated with tear-stained, single-spaced and unpublishable manuscripts about the deaths of husbands, children, parents . . . One girl said that what she really wanted to do was to write about her father's death in the sky so everyone could see.

My own prescription to overcome the helpless feelings was to write about my father's death in *The Times*. Writing it down, getting it published and making it public gave me a much-needed feeling of control, almost as if I, as the writer of the piece, although not the architect of my father's death, was at least in the powerful position of being its chronicler. One of the reasons people need to talk so much about a death is because they suffer from compulsive feelings of wanting to take control, again and again and again. Telling people is not always just born out of a desire to talk things out, or a desire for sympathy, or as a way of getting the truth to sink, slowly, in. It's a way of clawing back the power into your life. You have no power over the death but you do have power over the story.

Bereaved people love reading about death, too. After my father's death I consumed book after book on the subject – books about miscarriages, stillbirths, suicides, it didn't really matter. As long as the book was about death and bereavement it was fine by me. I seized at anything to find coherence, to stop the feelings of being a ship at sea. There is a longing to find the experience ordered and charted. This is, of course, why books on grief are so welcome, in that they do try to make some kind of sense of it all. Perhaps they offer a list of grieving 'stages', perhaps, like this one, they grapple with different emotions under neat chapter headings; but that is why in the end they are often so unsatisfying – because to be absolutely honest about grief you have to admit that there is no pattern, no one way, no two or even three ways, not necessarily any emotion even, perhaps just dreadful headaches and emptiness. There is no certainty about anything at all. All we can do is our best either to fight the feelings – or get the courage to submit to them. Or to accept that we either have none or can't bear to feel them.

Powerlessness is felt particularly acutely by children, who are so often not encouraged to talk or take part fully in a death. Unless kindly handled, children at a funeral may be upset for reasons entirely different from those that adults assume. Children feel powerless because they are surrounded by big friends of their relations, many of whom they have never met. If a parent has died, they feel they can't turn to their other parent for support in case talking about it upsets them; and they may often be thwarted in their efforts to remember actively what they loved about the person who died, or to talk openly about the death. And yet they have to remain listening passively to other people talking about the deceased. No wonder, too, that because their sense of powerlessness is so great, their sense of guilt can be so huge. Often children even feel responsible for their parent's or sibling's death, and this feeling may dog them for the rest of their lives.

And here we have it. *Enter guilt*, the most seductive and destructive of balms. On the heels of powerlessness, guilt steps in like a devil disguised as a kindly friend – because the phrase 'if only' in itself implies that *something could have been done to prevent it*. Guilt stands grinning on the shore of powerlessness, throwing out a faulty lifebelt and beckoning at you to grab it – even though once you have hold you will find that it drags you down even lower than before. 'The worst thing was not knowing, at first, how he died,' said the mother of a boy killed on a motorcycle.

Was it his fault? Could it have been prevented? For a while the police thought another car might have been involved, a hit and run accident. Then I was furious at the idea that someone should have killed him. But it was almost worse when the police ruled that possibility out. They said he had almost certainly lost control on a bend and gone into a tree. It was at this point, when there was no one to blame, that I nearly cracked up. My brother told me that I might start to feel guilty, and I shouldn't, but I completely forgot his warning. Guilt crept over me three nights after he died. It was almost a relief, you know. I wept and wept, wishing and wishing I had never allowed him a bike, or at least done more to discourage him from riding it. Despite what everyone says about it not being my fault, I don't think I will ever be able to forgive myself.

If you had started your partner smoking and, when he wanted to give it up, discouraged him because it made him so fat and ratty, then indeed you might, were he to die of lung cancer, have a good case for arguing: 'If only . . .' But bereaved people sing the 'If only' song even when the person who has died was a hundred years old and died simply of old age. 'If only' is a lullaby that offers hideous comfort, to soften the terrible truth: when death comes we are powerless. There was nothing, nothing at all, that we could have done to prevent it.

And yet how willingly we fly to guilt's welcoming arms! We are not powerless after all. No – it was *our fault!* Phew, what a relief!

Anthony Misiolek lost his daughter in the M40 minibus crash; she died partly because there were no seat-belts in the bus. And who does Mr Misiolek partly blame for this? Why, himself, of course. 'I should have delved into how my daughter was travelling, seen that it was really top mark,' he said, when interviewed by Julia Llewellyn Smith in *The Times*. 'But I didn't.' As if anyone in their right mind 'delves into' how their daughter travels when in the care of their school.

Since they have complete responsibility over their children's lives when they're young, parents of children who die often feel needlessly guilty about their deaths. Often they can spend years trying to claw control back into their lives by exonerating their misguided guilt, either by becoming overprotective of other children, or spearheading the kinds of campaigns that are headlined in newspapers: 'IT MUST NEVER HAPPEN AGAIN.'

Misplaced guilt has spurred some wonderful achievements. Suzy Lamplugh's mother set up the Suzy Lamplugh Trust – an organization to help working women protect themselves against the sort of man who must have murdered her daughter; one couple, whose son had been killed skiing in his early twenties, set up a charity to help young people train in sport; friends and relatives of a writer who died young offered a yearly prize for young authors; Colin and Wendy Parry, the parents of Tim Parry who died of injuries inflicted by an IRA bomb attack in Warrington, went on a courageous trip to both Northern Ireland and the Republic to talk with church representatives, politicians and ordinary people about the situation.

Those who can't assuage, by positive action, the usually unjustified feelings of guilt may get stuck with feelings of self-torment. Rather than risk the potential madness that might come from submitting themselves to feelings of powerlessness, their subconscious takes some cruel internal decision that it is better, however painful, to take responsibility for the death. These are the people who get stuck with the familiar bereavement cry of 'If only' echoing back at them again and again and again. 'If only' they had got a better doctor sooner, their loved one would not have died. 'If only' they hadn't asked their friends to supper, they would never have got involved in that fatal car crash.

Blake Morrison describes what happened after his father died.

My mother and I sit by the fire with plates on our knees. We drink wine with the roast chicken, and she begins a litany of *if onlys*: if only my father had had himself checked out regularly; if only he'd not refused the barium meal they'd offered him a month ago; if only she'd not had her accident.

'But the doctor thinks the secondaries have been there two years,' I say.

'Yes, I know, but if only they'd caught it a bit earlier, he'd have been spared that month of terrible pain.'

'But if he'd have known for that much longer,' I say, 'he'd have been devastated.'

'Yes . . . But if only he hadn't got so weak before the operation, maybe he'd have more fight.'

And Daphne du Maurier, writing on death and widowhood for Cruse, was not spared guilty feelings.

Like Emily Brontë, one of my first reactions after the first bewildered fits of weeping was to blame myself. I could have done more during the last illness, I should have observed, with sharp awareness, the ominous signs. I should have known, the last week, the last days, that his eyes followed me with greater intensity, and instead of moving about the house on trivial business, as I did, never left his side. How heartless, in retrospect, my last good night, when he murmured to me 'I can't sleep' and I kissed him and said 'You will, darling, you will' and went from the room. Perhaps if I had sat with him all night, the morning would have been otherwise. As it was, when morning came, and the nurses who had shared his vigil expressed some anxiety about his pallor and asked me to telephone the doctor, I went through to him expecting possibly an increase of weakness, but inevitably the usual smile. Instead . . . he turned his face to me, and died.

Interestingly, those who might feel guilty at having played a real part in someone's death, but with their consent, do not often feel guilty. I never felt a moment's guilt about my mother's death, despite the fact that I had begged the doctor to give her a final injection. My friend of eighty who was in excruciating pain had pleaded with me to get a book on DIY death from the Voluntary Euthanasia Society. I had not only done so, I had also advised her on everything from pill-grinding, to plastic bags, to where the note should be left – and I didn't feel an ounce of guilt when she finally succeeded in killing herself. But I still feel anger and guilt about my best friend who, at twenty-five, killed *herself* with an overdose without consulting me. I feel guilt because I had no control, and guilt is my stupid way of fooling myself that I did.

Suicide, of course, carries its own terrible form of guilt. For the suicide does seem to be saying that even the love of his closest friends and relations isn't strong enough to keep him wanting to stay alive; even the thought of their pain doesn't deter him. Suicides seem to be saying to the world and, specifically, to their friends and relatives: 'Fuck you!'

Despite the fact that it is no longer a criminal act, suicide is still seen as shameful. When one person wrote to a coroner who had given an open verdict on her brother's death, to ask him to reopen the inquest, she got back the accusatory answer: 'I'm very surprised that you even want to bring out the fact that your brother perhaps might have committed suicide.'

People who survive those who die of AIDS, particularly if they have been lovers, may feel guilty, however wrongly, that they might have transmitted the disease; sometimes the survivor feels stigmatized by his association with the victim, and in some cases sex and death can become confused, ending up with such guilt that the survivors' sex-lives fail completely. 'I have become completely impotent since Andrew died,' said one man whose partner died of AIDS.

I'm not HIV positive myself, but for some reason I feel responsible for Andrew's death. Everyone says he contracted it himself, but he always said he was faithful and before he died we never talked about where he got it from. Perhaps I've become impotent because it's easier to believe it was my fault that Andrew died than to face up to the fact that he might have been unfaithful. I still can't really understand it. I know you can't catch AIDS off lavatory seats, but as we did everything together there was really no way he could have screwed anyone else. I keep having tests, because I feel sure there must be some mistake. I can't understand how I don't have it. I mean, I would have caught it from him, anyway. I am fairly sure I am HIV positive, despite what the doctors say. Actually I don't really know what I feel.

Misplaced guilt is frequently felt by mothers of miscarriages or stillborn children. They take all the blame themselves. Perhaps it was an old abortion they had that was responsible; perhaps it was the fact that a few years back they didn't even want a family and that this death was punishment for their thoughts. Perhaps it was a particular kind of sex agreed to with their partners, perhaps it was an aspirin, or the fact that they flew in an aeroplane or dug a hole to plant a bulb; perhaps they jogged, or danced, or smoked one cigarette. Whatever, the thought that perhaps the miscarriage just happened, that it was fate, is an intolerable one. It is easier to feel like a murderer than to feel like a victim.

Even when people aren't feeling directly guilty about causing a death, they often feel generalized guilt that just hangs around like poison gas. How many of us have told someone else that they'll be the death of us, how many of us have actually wished another person dead? The line: 'You just wish I'd disappear, don't you!' yelled in a drunken argument ten years ago can suddenly rise up like a drowned body from a stagnant pond, the words ringing in the ears of a guilty survivor like some creepy premonition from Nostradamus.

I felt guilty for being unable to see my father before he died. Would he have had a special message for me? Was there something he could have said that would have made sense of my life and my past? Could he, in five visiting minutes, have perhaps explained, just by a look, our highly complicated relationship? Would he have given me the answer, the secret? I feel guilty for not seeing him, not so much for not telling him I loved him because I had, once, much to his intense embarrassment and I wasn't going to say it again, but because I wonder if by not visiting him I perhaps deprived him of the chance of telling me that he loved me.

Toby Young, in an article in the *Mail on Sunday* entitled 'Am I Emotionally Incorrect?', got his guilty feelings over in advance. He was lucky enough to be able to squeeze in the words he wanted to say to his dying mother in time.

> When she was dying – she died of cancer – I was acutely conscious of the need to 'clear the air'. Nothing in particular, just the usual stuff: apologize for being such an awful son, assure her I'd be nicer to my sister, tell her I loved her. But I knew that saying these things was solely for my benefit. That is, I wanted to tell her things that I knew I'd regret not telling her; I wanted to avoid future guilt.

Then there is the guilt felt when one partner dies in a relationship that was not always happy. Despite the fact that she was married to the most irritating man in the world, whose nature would have tried the patience of a saint, my friend tormented herself with the fact that she had been impatient with him. She should never have been so snappy and tetchy. She should have told him more often that she loved him. And during a bad relationship there is so much anger, often unspoken, that the survivor may really convince him or herself that their thoughts were responsible. The result of this is that the dead person is usually idealized to sainthood to compensate for all the ghastly things the survivor thought about them when they were alive. The survivor may buy enormous wreaths and spend fortunes on coffins in order to balance all the bad things they used to think or say.

Some survivors even feel guilty about being happy. They castigate themselves for having got over the death too quickly, or for not feeling sad enough. 'Bereavement is bad enough without adding to your distress by having guilt feelings about not mourning enough,' wrote Dr R.M. Youngson in *Grief: Rebuilding Your Life after a Bereavement*. 'The intensity of your grief is a measure of the seriousness of your loss, not a measure of the virtue of the one who has died. Your loss has to do with many things beside that. The one who has died has not suddenly become a saint.'

The bereaved may feel guilty about having money to spend at last, or enjoying themselves. Some people may even feel guilty simply for being alive. In *OM – An Indian Pilgrimage*, Geoffrey Moorhouse wrote about how he felt after his daughter had died of cancer at seventeen 'just as she was beginning to realize how marvellous life could be. That day I thought I would never smile again. But gradually we all came to terms with losing Brigie and got on with living . . .' Four years later he had a spectacular heart attack and was only saved by a couple of amazing flukes. Indeed, after crashing his car, a policeman said he should be given up for dead. Because of astonishingly coincidental intervention by a policewoman and ambulanceman who just happened to be nearby, he survived. But after that he was consumed by guilt.

But why? Why had I been brought back from the dead to enjoy yet another helping at the age of fifty-three, when Brigie had scarcely been allowed time to appreciate how wonderful life could be – for everyone but her? I was unable to escape a feeling that I had been given, had virtually robbed her of, what was rightfully hers. The longer I lived the more I was tormented by a profound feeling of guilt, sometimes breaking down embarrassingly on hearing a tune, reading a phrase, seeing a gesture that connected these two terminals in my life and shattered me . . .

When guilt gets too much, or the 'If onlys' scream too loudly, it can be worth turning the idea on its head. If only he or she had lived – what then? 'My religious belief helped me much more than I would have dared to count on,' wrote the woman whose daughter died of anorexia.

Because I do not believe that this life is the whole story, my main concern was that Edie should have all the help possible in her next existence, whatever that may be. Phone calls and telegrams soon contacted the people I felt could help, and then when I knew of all the prayers and services that had been said for her, I felt surprisingly relieved. I really did feel that she was being well looked-after. With this came the conviction that whatever her purpose in life was, it had been achieved. It didn't ease the pain of our losing her, but it made me feel quite positive in my reply to the many people who felt her life had been a waste. In terms of what might have been – perhaps 'what might have been' might have been a lifetime of torture. One can't speculate on that.

Guilt, for whatever reason, and however understandable, is a completely negative emotion. It is an emotion like a wasting disease. If we lurk in the valley of guilt too long, we become bitter and stuck, tormenting ourselves with our mistaken belief in our own power. True, had we taken different action, the dead person might have lived an hour or two longer; similarly, he might have died quicker. Or he might have survived in agony. And why is guilt – this distorted power – never balanced by grandiose self-congratulatory feelings? If we persist in feeling guilty about what we did not do, then surely, if there is any sense in it at all, we should be patting ourselves on the back for what we did do – for the moments, perhaps, when we saved the lives of our loved ones by prompt action, the time we cried: 'Watch out!' when they were overtaking on a dangerous bend, or simply when we nurtured them with love and good advice.

But there is, of course, no sense in it. We can spend our lives doing a kind of gloomy penance, swearing we will never love again, or refusing to emerge from our misery, seeing our grief and torment as a kind of sackcloth and ashes tribute to the person we lost. But it's not really. We are actually punishing ourselves for something we feel we were responsible for. And it is only when we start turning the blame away from ourselves that guilt starts dissolving.

But as we turn the blame away, where is it to go? Who *is* to blame? After all, we've got to blame someone, haven't we? I mean, it's only natural. The idea that the blow came out of the sky, as it were, is just too unbearable. To cope with that would involve some kind of acceptance, and that would be frightful, and make it seem as if we didn't mind, when we do. So, if we weren't responsible, if we didn't do it, then someone, something, must have *done this to us*. Stands to reason, doesn't it? And thus we may (but always remember we may not) turn from experiencing the feelings of powerlessness and guilt, to finding within us the least acceptable emotion of bereavement of all – rage.

5. Rage

I experienced the most intense anger, bitterness and pain which raced through every part of me, and I shouted a host of expletives. My anger was directed not just at the evil creatures who had planted the bomb but at the injustice of Tim losing such a promising young life. My rage was also born out of the fact that I would never hear him again, that he and I would never embrace again ... (Colin Parry in *Tim – An Ordinary Boy*, on hearing that his son would almost certainly have to be taken off his life-support machine)

Those who have felt nothing but sadness on the death of a friend or relative will feel, as I used to do, rather offended by the idea that anger is considered an integral part of bereavement. Anger is an unwelcome guest at the wake, and one for which most of us are completely unprepared. But even those who don't experience major outbursts will, if they are honest, usually acknowledge its presence somewhere, even at the most minor level.

'I do think the vicar could have got the choristers to put on their white surplices instead of just singing in their anoraks. It looked so tacky ...' 'It was not just a shame that she couldn't come to the funeral, it was simply inconsiderate ...' 'How dare his old school send him information about an old boys' reunion when they *must* have read about his death in the papers ...' 'The man at the bank had the nerve to request my husband's signature on our joint account cheque even though he must have *known* ...' 'All she said was: "I'm so sorry" and then not a word more ...' Most bereaved people will find these kinds of petty resentments quite familiar. I even managed to dredge up some anger when my mother died, even though I was incredibly relieved for both our sakes that she had finally gone. I got masses of letters from her grateful students saying what a wonderful teacher she had been, and how they would not have got where they were today had it not been for her brilliant encouragement. But was I grateful? No. I tore them up spitting tacks. It was all very well for them to say what a wonderful teacher she'd been. But what about me? Did she have any time for me? No. Not a mention of how much she had loved *me*. No, the letters all seemed to be about how she had loved *them*. It all seemed most unfair.

I'm not implying that those letters weren't well-meant and kindly felt; I only mention them to illustrate how easy it is for an angry bereaved person to take offence from even the most sympathetic words and actions. It's small wonder, considering this, that friends cross to the other side of the street when they see a bereaved person coming their way. They may be embarrassed and not know what to say; but they are also frightened that some of the bereaved person's flak may come their way and smack them in the face.

Rebecca Abrams wrote about how irritated she got with all the kindly people who were pottering about eager to help. She felt angry with the lot of them. There were too many, they were wittering on, bringing meals, chatting tritely about her stepfather. 'If only they'd go home and leave us alone,' she thought.

One reason why funeral directors may talk in hushed voices, as if the widow or widower were asleep, is so they don't provoke hostility in their clients. They don't wish to be the bearers of the bad news. But if this is so, their tactics rarely work; undertakers soak up a lot of aggression from the bereaved. 'He came in this ghastly suit with his ghastly hushed voice, talking about my "other half", can you imagine!' 'His bill was exorbitant!' 'They never even asked me about the flowers . . .!' Even BUPA caught the lash of my widower friend's anger. 'They sent me my new registration today. I was shattered to see that my status has been changed to "single" and wrote to them requesting it be amended to "widower". I said that "single" seemed to wipe out at a stroke the fact of forty-nine years of close and loving marriage.'

Similarly the eulogies about the dead person prevent the bereaved from feeling rage against those who talk about the

departed. The exhortation 'Never speak ill of the dead' is made
not because God thinks it's bad to be unpleasant about dead
people; it's either because if you do utter a word of criticism,
one of the bereaved relatives will get you round the throat and
try to kill you, or, worse, that once you open your mouth to say
anything critical about a much-loved lost person, you might
never stop, your bitter judgements spewing out of your mouth
like toads. Bereavement, after all, feels like a betrayal of trust,
and naturally the people left behind are hopping mad at being, as
it feels to them, conned and cheated.

I have found it very hard to speak about my father's weak-
nesses to my other relatives; I can feel antagonism rise in them,
even though I knew him longer than any of them. ('Even
though I knew him longer than any of them . . .' Do I detect a
tinge of scalding bitterness still? What brought on those
uncalled-for last ten words that just snuck quietly into the prose?
Even now, writing, I thought, reasonably calmly about anger
three years after my father's death, I can't help sparks of hot fat
flying up from the flaming pan of loss.)

At funeral rituals, the American Indians used to shoot spears
and arrows into the sky, and at military funerals guns are still
fired, in an apparent expression of fury. Woe betide you if you
happen to catch a stray bullet. And it's interesting that Dylan
Thomas's poem is so often quoted at funerals:

> Do not go gentle into that good night
> Rage, rage against the dying of the light.

In these two lines, the poet exhorts his father, who is about to
die, to resist death. It is completely inappropriate to quote it at
funerals with its 'please don't die' sentiment. But of course it is
quoted because it fits the mood of the bereaved so perfectly.
Those two words 'Rage, rage' – those are what the bereaved
want to hear at funeral services, to express their *own* fury at
death.

Raging at the person who has died is one of the most
common and illogical, surprising and unfair directions of anger.

Forget society finding this an unacceptable emotion; those who experience it may feel incredibly confused and guilty as well. In one survey of bereaved people, 8 per cent expressed anger at the dead person. One man kept his wife's ashes in his bedroom and shouted at them. Another screamed abuse at his wife while sitting on her gravestone. In *In the Springtime of the Year*, by Susan Hill, Ruth's husband, Ben, is killed by a tree.

> She had talked to Ben, too, because he was still there, wasn't he, just behind her shoulder, at the end of the landing, on the other side of a door, and it was sometimes just ordinary talk, she might only say, 'Hello Ben'. But for the rest of the time, she blamed him, screamed out in resentment, 'Where are you? Where are you? Why did you have to die? Oh, why did you die?'

Rebecca Abrams described how, when her father died, her rage was vented, completely inappropriately, on her stepfather. She started to overeat and be rude and aggressive to him and 'family mealtimes were soon unbearable with me picking fights and flying into a rage at the slightest provocation ... Much of the rage I directed at my stepfather was, I later realized, fury with my father for having died and hurt me – and anger with myself for not having been able to prevent his death.'

Suicide brings out the worst anger in those left behind. And with good reason. My mother tried to commit suicide twice, unsuccessfully. She once left a note. 'Darling. I'm sorry. I do love you – Mummy.' The letter made me just as angry as if she had died. Talk about mixed messages. I do love you. But I'm going to leave you. One of those statements could not be true, and since actions speak louder than words I knew which one was the lie.

Of course when people do succeed there is the fury of being left, at feeling rejected, punished for not caring enough. 'I could kill you for killing yourself' is a common reaction. These vicious feelings are not just restricted to suicides, however. For often we see people's deaths over which they have no control as *kinds* of suicides. We feel, irrationally, 'If you had really wanted to hang on, you could have done. Despite the fact that you were a million years old and dying of cancer, you left us because you didn't really love us.'

Not all rage is directed at the person who has died, though. There is another kind of fury, a free-floating anger, turning the bereaved person into a loose cannon, surprising even himself with his random discharges of unfocused rage – at bus conductors, shop assistants, partners, children and all manner of innocent bystanders. Or he may become eaten up with repressed fury, experiencing explosive feelings in his head as if he were going mad. Or the anger may find a clear, but usually irrational, focus on someone else suffering the same bereavement.

'After my mother died I was furious with my stepfather, though thankfully he never knew it,' wrote one woman.

I would wake in the middle of the night thinking about him, filled with loathing. I would sit in a chair addressing him, citing everything he had done in the past to upset me. My whispered voice would grow hoarse with rage as tears poured down my cheeks. And when I had got up to the present day I would simply start again. Take Two. 'To start with – you did this, you didn't do that . . . you didn't want me home for Christmas, you forgot my birthday, you took her away on holiday when I was ill . . .' And so it would go on, for hours sometimes, until I was burned out. In the morning my mood might have changed. What had I been fussing about? He was only human, after all. He had nice sides to him. He was unhappy, too. I would ring him up solicitously, just to check he hadn't been harmed by the evil rays I'd been shooting out in the early hours of the morning. I was terrified by the depth of my feelings. I have never in my life felt such rage and loathing before. Now I look back I think I was reliving the rage I didn't feel when my mother married again. Her death brought back memories of when she'd been taken from me before, and my stepfather became suddenly an easy target for all the loss connected with my mother, even those losses he wasn't responsible for.

Anger may be directed at those even further away. Doctors are often targets for rage. 'It was just the expression on his face when he told me my sister had died,' said one woman.

Nothing. I didn't feel he cared a jot. I know he'd been unavailable when they had tried to get him the night before, and they had to get another doctor. I am certain if he had been around my sister might have been saved. I really think he killed her, and quite frankly I would like to kill him. I wrote an anonymous note to the hospital about him and one night I even put a spell on him that I found in a book.

All the peripheral characters around a death – undertakers' assistants, priests, florists, printers, organists, solicitors, bank managers – they all come in for flak. 'The priest who presided over my father's memorial service simply left out the one prayer I particularly wanted in,' said one woman, who still remembers the hurt even though her father died ten years ago. 'And immediately after the service he hopped on his bicycle and raced away without so much as a shaken hand or a pat on the back. How could any man behave like that?'

'The vicar we had at the crematorium didn't even get my wife's name right,' complained a widower.

She was known all her life as 'Ronnie' and he called her 'Veronica'. I suppose it was because that was her name on the death certificate. But you would think he could have checked, wouldn't you? They must come across this all the time, but they never bother. I have never felt right after that funeral. It was as if they buried a different woman.

Hospital nurses are another easy target. It's been reported that people can often slope out of the hospital after their close relative has died, full of toadying thanks and heartfelt gratitude about how wonderful the nurses have been – and then return a few minutes later, storming into the ward raging that someone has stolen the dead person's pyjamas.

Lowly clerks who operate computers may find hatred and loathing heaped upon their heads if they make the mistake of sending out a letter to a dead person – a perfectly normal error and not one to get really fussed about. But these mistakes often make big-headlined news stories in papers. 'GAS MEANIES HUNT DOWN MAN IN GRAVE! "They sent my dead son a bill for £47.50!" sobbed a sixty-year-old widow, whose son passed away last week after a long illness,' is the usual gist, followed by a tale that implies that the gas company sent the letter out deliberately, knew all along, were no better than grave-robbers, and deserved to be sued till they squeaked.

A woman whose husband died of a brain tumour at forty-seven said:

> The thing I found hard to deal with was the finances. David had always organized things. There were so many well-meaning people giving advice, but I didn't know who to trust. What made me really angry were the bank and other financial institutions. I told the bank about his death, but three weeks later a cheque book arrived for him. One firm even sent a letter to him about life insurance!

Certainly I remember every single bereavement slight as fresh as if it were yesterday. The world of death seemed peopled by cold and uncaring people from cruel service industries, deliberately putting in orange flowers when I'd asked for white, asking for cash in advance rather than accepting a cheque. Even after years and years I still feel hatred and loathing for these unsympathetic creatures. Or were they unsympathetic? Probably not. They are just targets for my anger.

When her stepfather died, Rebecca Abrams felt furious about his obituary, which read that he was 'mourned by his widow and four children'. What about her and her brother, she asked herself? He had looked after them, too. 'Was our grief to be dismissed so easily?' Jeremy Howe, whose wife, Dr Elizabeth Howe, was murdered, said of his daughter: 'After Lizzie's death she was like a loose cannon ... incredibly temperamental. When I was interviewing possible nannies she'd go up and hit them.'

Unfocused anger is perhaps the worst of all to bear because it is so burdensome and unpredictable. It is like heaving around a load of shit encased in an extremely thin bag, one that is liable to split at any time. The fear of disclosing what is in the bag forces progress to be very slow, conversation to be extremely measured. When my father died, I wrote in my diary: 'For some reason since then I have been feeling completely mad, bursting with rage, I can almost feel myself eating myself up with fury inside, like a cannibal who is eating herself.' Another bereaved woman wrote, after her partner had died: 'After the continual weeping in the summer came fits of rage. I threw my body around and grovelled in anguish. I took to hurling things around and beating myself continually against walls. I would pound my fits into beds and pillows, screaming with rage.'

'Rage creeps up on you unawares, too,' wrote Mary Stott in the *Guardian*, after the death of her husband. 'I was coming back from London and as I walked along a crowded compartment and saw people laughing and talking and reading and sleeping, something in my mind went briefly out of gear. Their normality was hideous to me. I was in hostile country, an enemy alien.'

An obvious target for anger is, of course, God. After my father's death I found myself blaming God a lot, and I didn't even believe in him to start with. However, Voltaire's quote that 'If God didn't exist it would be necessary to invent Him' really came into its own. I did have to invent him. He was needed – as a punch-bag.

A woman who lost her newborn son described a funeral service where a vicar made a speech along the lines of the boy's death being quite a good thing because through it I would find God. Now I'm not strongly religious but this finally disillusioned me. He made up some silly parables about people finding God through suffering and thanking God for it: I thought, 'Oh, yes, well if that is how God acts, I don't want to know.' It may be very blasphemous but I'd rather have my baby than find God I'm afraid.

After a miscarriage, one woman wrote: 'I felt particularly angry with God: I felt depressed the following morning in hospital and the tears were rolling.' A sister came and told her the miscarriage was God's way of getting rid of mistakes. 'All the time she was talking there was a mongol girl in the ward yelling her head off and I thought "If that's God's idea of perfection it's time he went back to school."'

Whether we go to church or not, the idea of God inevitably pops into most people's minds when they're bereaved. Suddenly we remember something about 'God giveth life and he taketh it away.' And all of a sudden there is no mystery to death at all. Or rather, about as much mystery as finding Jo Bloggs covered in blood at the scene of a murder, surrounded by a million witnesses who could point the finger at him and say he did it. But when God goes on trial, a beatific barrister with a clerical collar rolls up and starts arguing in his defence. And how does the defence run? Surprise alibis? Contradictory medical evidence? No. The sum total of the argument is simply: 'It's a big mystery.' But to the God is Guilty brigade, it is no mystery at all. Who did it? God did it. He is guilty as charged. Why he did it is of course a mystery, but most bereaved people don't care about the whys. Bad God. Slam him in jail. Throw away the key. What makes the whole thing even worse is the Christian idea that we are his children, and God is there to look after us. So not only does he murder us in our beds, but when we turn to him for comfort he is either not around or claiming it wasn't him who did it. He is not just a murderer, he is a Myra Hindley of a murderer, someone who, by his nature, sets himself up to care for people, and then betrays their trust. Small wonder that some believers leave the church when people die.

In my diary, after my father had died, I wrote:

> I burst into tears on my way to work and felt so utterly furious with life that when Denis rang me I couldn't speak, I just said that I hoped I was never reincarnated and if I ever did get to some kind of spirit world and anyone asked me if I wanted to go back to earth or not I definitely would not put my tick in the box, and I'd also make sure that I was not put on the mailing list. And if I *had* to go back I'd be certain to put myself at the back of the queue. What on earth was the point of all that loving when it's just broken? God is like a football hooligan, just destructive.

I was amazed to read that C. S. Lewis had just the same feelings:

> Meanwhile, where is God? When you are happy, so happy that you have no sense of needing Him ... and turn to Him with gratitude and praise, you will be – or so it feels – welcomed with open arms. But go to Him when your need is desperate, when all other help is vain, and what do you find? A door slammed in your face, and a sound of bolting and double bolting on the inside. After that, silence. You may as well turn away ... There are no lights in the windows. It might be an empty house ...

He added:

> Not that I am (I think) in much danger of ceasing to believe in God. The real danger is of coming to believe such dreadful things about Him. The conclusion I dread is not: 'So there's no God after all' but 'So this is what God's really like. Deceive yourself no longer.'

Clerics argue that it's quite natural to blame God. But they claim that God isn't the root of all evil, pain, illness and suffering; rather he's there to help us through such suffering. But Christian faith is a faith of hope, and it's very difficult to accommodate this hope with grief. The doctrine of immortality and resurrection makes grieving more difficult, and the added problem with Christianity is that it tends to want people to smile. Acceptance is not a big deal in Christianity; nor is fury; but 'love your neighbour' is.

In Susan Hill's *In the Springtime of the Year* the widow, Ruth, cries out to God: '"Why did you give it to me, if you were going to take it away? Why did you give me Ben and then kill him?" And she did not know who she was accusing, God or not-God, life or death, or Ben himself.' The same sense of betrayal was felt by Blake Morrison who, in *And When Did You Last See Your Father?*, concluded: 'Never to have loved seems best: love means two people getting too close; it means people wanting to be with each other all the time, and leaving the other bereft.'

Even religious people can be tormented with doubts. When, later, in *In the Springtime of the Year*, the curate's child dies, he, too, is beset with similar rage against the Almighty. He says:

'I should leave here. I should resign from Holy Orders and go away from this place. What right have I to stay now?'
'Because your child died?'
'Because she has died and now I know that everything I believed in and lived for has died with her. Because my life is a lie, I am a lie. How can I visit them, people sick, people dying and in distress, needing truth, what have I to say to them? How can I hold services in the church and preach and pray and know that it is all a lie? I used to know what words to say, but there are no words and there is no help for anyone.'

Ruth tries to comfort him, saying that there are things she now understands about death that she didn't understand at the time, but his reply is adamant.

'How could there be anything to understand? There was no meaning to it. Your husband was young and fit, and a good man, he was happy, you were happy, and then he was dead, and now my child is dead, and there is only cruelty, there is no purpose in any of it. It means *nothing*.'

A child's death almost certainly means that the bereaved parents will feel rage. Worst, of course, when it is directed at each other. After her daughter died from meningitis, a friend wrote:

Of course we have changed. Sudden quarrels and rage flashed between my husband and me, as the undertaker who arranged my daughter's funeral free because he, too, had lost a daughter, told us it would. This is normal. Grief is an enraging business. It leads to misunderstanding and splits many couples apart unless they are prepared for it.

Rage is a pretty antisocial emotion at the best of times, even when it is directed against deserving targets. Maybe most people have better and more understanding friends than I do, but I learned that even my closest friends found it hard to put up with the diatribes about doctors, hospitals, vicars, relations and God that I fed them over the phone. They tried to reason with me, to calm me down, when all I wanted was for them to agree with me, however irrational my rage-filled arguments may have been. Rage, anger, fury – these are not things easily shared. Friends much prefer to hear you crying down the phone than spewing bile. They would prefer that you rang up saying you wanted to kill yourself and could they help, than hear you crazed with bitterness, resentfulness and vengeful thoughts about, probably, completely innocent people.

Small wonder, then, that most people keep their evil feelings to themselves, festering inside or leaking out in insidiously destructive ways. Small wonder that they often repress the feelings completely, springing on them with both feet and hurtling into mad eulogies about their loved ones. Rather than rage against the dead person, they fantasize about how marvellous they were; rather than express their fury, they spend fortunes on the funeral to disguise the intensity of their angry feelings. They talk only of the dead person's good points, they won't have a word heard

against them, they cry, they worship at the feet of the dead one
... then they often get ill and think: 'And now I get ill! On top
of everything else!' when in fact they are ill with repressed anger
and loathing.

And yet not all feelings of grief and loss are simply anger
turned inwards. Most painful feelings stem from real feelings of
sadness. But disentangling our muddled emotions one from
another is pretty much an impossible task. Just hanging on in
there is about the best that most of us can manage. Getting
through a bereavement is like riding a bucking bronco. The
saddle is no place to sit quietly and contemplate which feelings
are anger turned inward and which are grief and sorrow.

No, it's all we can do to keep our fingers gripped to its mane.
And just hope we don't fall off.

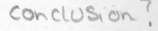

Conclusion?

6. *Misery ...*

> There lies behind everything, and you can believe this or not as you
> wish, a certain quality which we may call grief. It's always there, just
> under the surface, just behind the façade, sometimes very nearly ex-
> posed, so that you can see simply the shape of it as you can see
> sometimes through the surface of an ornamental pond on a still day,
> the dark, gross, inhuman outline of a carp gliding slowly past; when
> you realize suddenly that the carp were always there, below the sur-
> face, even while the water sparkled in the sunshine, and while you
> patronized the quaint ducks and the supercilious swans, the carp
> were down there, unseen. It bides its time, this quality ... The name
> of this quality is grief ... *Grief*; the word is grief; the dark centre of
> life, the incommunicable, the deaf-mute who sits behind the mind,
> watching it pretend, not even bothering to mock; biding its time.
> (James Saunders, *Next Time I'll Sing to You*)

Sadness and misery may strike at any time. Sooner than you
think. Later than you think. Or not at all. True, some people
start crying the moment they hear of the death, and continue
for weeks; some don't cry but are felled by a deep, unyielding
axe of sheer depression, loneliness and misery. I say 'can' and
'some' advisedly; the idea that everyone cries a lot and feels
miserable after a death is, as I have said before, an idea bathed in
as much fantasy as is the idea of romantic love. Not everybody
feels grief and sadness. They can, instead, feel simply 'terrible'
for a long period. And even in cases where the bereaved do feel
grief, it certainly doesn't always come at the 'right' time, whenever that may be. It may be delayed, sometimes for years. For
instance, a woman who loses her husband may remain dry-eyed
while she still has her husband's loving Alsatian to look after.
How very brave she is, say her friends. (How very cold, they
think.) But when the Alsatian dies, all hell is let loose. (And how
very weird she is, too, think her friends, crying more over a dog
than over her husband!) But although she is ostensibly crying

over the Alsatian, perhaps she has cunningly delayed the grief she felt for her husband and transferred the feelings she had for him on to her dog. When the dog dies – the balloon goes up.

And anyway, what are we grieving for? Usually a million and one things, of which only one is the actual person who has died. One man's father died, and the loss left him cold. He thought nothing of it. But six weeks later the family gardener died, of whom he had been very fond. He was beside himself. He was also beside himself with confusion and shame, because his grief seemed so utterly inappropriate. But was he in fact grieving for his father when he mourned the gardener? Or was he crying over what his father wasn't – crying over the fact that here was a lovely old man who had nurtured the plants and the earth in a way his father had never nurtured him? Was he crying about the loss of a father he had *never actually had*? Or – and so often one overlooks the obvious – was he simply crying over the gardener more because he loved him more?

When my father died I found myself crying for all kinds of funny old losses and deaths I'd not remembered being too upset about before. Driving back from clearing out the cottage he owned in the country I started to cry – not for my father, but for my friend who had committed suicide twenty years before and for whom I had never really cried. My father's death brought back the memory of other deaths; but at the same time, future losses brought back his death. When my son left home six months later to go round India before university I was distraught; when I lost my job three months after that I felt suicidal. It was as if all these smaller, later losses were like hammer blows on a recent bruise, rendering me quite helpless, even though I might have coped quite successfully with each one had its timing been different. Each loss – *including my father's death* – brought back memories of other older losses; and certainly people who have suffered loss of any kind in their childhood, and who have not properly resolved their feelings, or managed at least to put the episodes properly behind them, feel perhaps most poignantly every single loss thereafter, each new loss hitting them like a bigger and bigger snowball, picking up more grief and horror on the way.

I realized this when another member of my family said, about my father: 'If only he would walk through that door!' It was then that it came home to me how little my grief was actually connected with his death. If he walked through that door, fine. It would have been extremely nice to see him. But I would *still* have felt dreadful, shocked, fearful, angry and full of unhappiness. I might even look to him to console me in my sadness. Because his loss, like a gong, had set up dreadful resonances from the past. In other words, had he arrived back and stopped the sound from his own gong of loss, the sound of the other gongs would still have been deafening.

The truth is that not all bereaved people who mourn are mourning the loss of the one who has died. It does seem that the more in tune you are with life, the more you live in the present day, the less emotional baggage you carry with you in your daily life, and the happier the relationship you had with whoever it was who died, the more easy, surprisingly, it is to feel sad – and then move on. But the more loss a relationship contained, and the more emotionally uncomfortable the bereaved person is with his own life anyway, the worse can be the effect of a death. 'My friend spent her life being really horrible and resentful about her mother, but when she died, and I said: "You must be relieved," she astounded me by bursting into tears. She really was desperately and genuinely unhappy,' said one woman.

Since people tend to mourn bad relationships more than good ones, and because of the confused feelings of guilt involved, they may over-compensate to make up for their bad feelings. But it could be, too, that the loss triggers off all kinds of old losses in their past. So it is possible to feel both – pleasure at seeing the back of the ghastly old father, say, who drove them nuts, but also sad because his going reminds them of other, more poignant, goings.

In *Crying with Laughter* Bob Monkhouse described how he felt on the death of his mother, with whom he had an extremely difficult relationship – if the hideous connection he described could ever be so called.

> When she died I felt no particular sense of loss for two or three weeks. Then Jackie [his wife] made some quite inconsequential remark in no way connected with my mother and it triggered my pent-up grief. I collapsed with sorrow and loss, grieving not so much for her death as for her life, racked with regret for the lack of all that could and should have existed between us. For several weeks afterwards my conversation was subject to lapses. I'd simply lose the hang of what I was saying and start to become uncontrollably distressed. Having to go onstage every evening in Bournemouth was a blessing. This may seem strange to you if you haven't experienced some similar relief from the oppression of bereavement.

We may be grieving over loss generally – grieving in the way that we all cry over *La Traviata*, because it reminds us of our own feelings of abandonment; or perhaps we are grieving over something quite different and selfish, about the loss of our own potential. In *Among the Dead*, Michael Tolkin's hero, Frank, finds he can hear nothing during the memorial service for his wife – not the prayers, the address, a baby's cry or even the trumpeters. But finally he tries to hear something – himself.

> The hell with it. With everything he could, he forced the air from his chest and his gut through a constricted throat, epiglottis engaged, and tried to make, without hearing, the loudest scream he could.

Frank started to cry. He was crying because he suddenly realized that he was only a dabbler in life.

> He knew no one would fault him for his misery so long as he didn't tell them that he cried now because he would never produce a record, never write a song that the world would sing, that he would always and only be a salesman.

He brought a hand up to cover his eyes, and before he closed them he could see that the people in the room were watching him, just as he had watched the other mourners in the room whose sadness had already erupted.

Who knows what people are feeling when they cry? We assume they cry for the dead person, but what is really going on in their heads? Sometimes we hardly know ourselves. Is it shock? Loneliness? A sense of our own inadequacy? Perhaps when people are bereaved most of the tears they shed are the ones they used to shed for their mothers when they were tiny.

Often it is not so much the person we mourn but the role they played in our lives. Anyone who has cared for someone sick mourns not only the passing of the person they were looking after, but also the loss of a full-time job. The death causes the most terrible void in their lives, which makes them feel not just unhappy but completely unwanted, useless, empty. The feeling of howling loneliness after a bereavement is unlike the loneliness felt at any other time. You feel you are just a speck in the universe; you may even feel that you yourself don't exist at all (one of the most frightening feelings in the world) because you always felt in the past that your existence was defined by the love of the one who now is dead.

When parents grieve for a child they grieve from two points of view – not just for the loss of the child, but empathetically, for the child losing its own parents. They also grieve for the loss of a potential future, and their own connection with it, they grieve for a loss of part of themselves and for the loss of their role as parent. This touching poem is written by someone who suffered a miscarriage, yet it describes everything that parents feel when they lose a child of any age:

> What have I lost?
> At 7 weeks an embryo about 8mm long,
> a large bulge where the heart is,
> a bump for a brain,
> dimples that will become ears,

> thickenings that will become eyes,
> buds where arms and legs are growing . . .
>
> The excitement of an expanding tummy,
> the overwhelming love holding a newborn,
> a strong sucking mouth eager for my milk,
> first smiles at 6 weeks,
> cute crawls at 8 months,
> cautious toddlers at one year,
> hugs and kisses,
> giggles and fun,
> and so much love,
> a child I will never know.
> Boy? Girl?
> So many hopes and dreams . . .
>
> this is what I've lost.

Others may grieve a lost future together, from the kind of future expected by this young mother, to a promising retirement together. All death involves a loss of promise, and all death involves acute disappointment.

After President Kennedy died, Alistair Cooke broadcast in *Letter from America*: 'I cannot remember a time, certainly in the last thirty years, when the people everywhere around you are so quiet, so tired-looking, and, for all the variety of their shape and colour and character, so plainly the victims of a huge and bitter disappointment.' He felt that they had been cheated of the promise of what people had begun to call the Age of Kennedy.

Disappointed. Cheated. No wonder we go round with grey faces or howl like babies.

We also feel lonely, because bereavement is a kind of abandonment. In *Living with Fear*, Professor Isaac Marks writes: 'Grief is a special kind of separation anxiety. Generally, it takes some time for people to accept the death of a loved one, and until they do, separation anxiety is marked.' And when a partner dies, we may not just feel sad because we miss their companionship; we may feel lonely because we lose all kinds of other things that they provided. In a partnership, we may have in some ways lived through them, basking in each other's glory. Or our partner may have played the role of mother, father, son, daughter, protector, provider, lame duck, ego-booster ... Any death of a close relative, from partner, to child, to parent, pushes us into a new role, and we miss the familiarity of our old one. But it's loneliness that prompts the tears, and it's small wonder that it's quite a common experience for the bereaved to feel overcome with inexpressible longings, if their loved one is buried, to get out there and actually dig him or her up. Bring him back! Why not? It's a perfectly natural primitive urge.

C.S. Lewis poignantly observed his own loneliness after his wife died. He had been a bachelor for a long time before enjoying a brief year of happiness, and he berated God: 'Oh God, God, why did you take such trouble to force this creature out of its shell if it is now doomed to crawl back – to be sucked back – into it?' Everything seemed pointless when there was no one to share it with or appreciate it. 'I loathe the slightest effort. Not only writing but even reading a letter is too much. Even shaving. What does it matter now whether my cheek is rough or smooth?'

Helen Osborne said she found her evenings unspeakable. 'The dogs sit for hours by John's chair and stare sorrowfully at it. John was so noisy. He was a great rattler around late at night. He loved loud music and he'd go around the house singing old music-hall songs.'

When my father died, loneliness hit me like a sledgehammer. The first thing I wanted to do when I heard the news of his death was to ring him up. He would have been astonished and sympathetic. 'Poor, poor you,' he would have said. 'How absolutely ghastly. Do come round when you want. And all those awful undertakers – and the funeral. And those vicars with their lizardy necks in too-big clerical collars and their oily smiles. I can't wait to hear about it!' The loneliness of knowing I couldn't share all the black stories of his funeral with him was far sadder than the funeral itself.

This is the loneliness of knowing that a hundred shared jokes are buried along with the death, and that a thousand little activities and understandings have gone up in smoke, things that in themselves, without the existence of the dead person, have no meaning at all. When her mother died, what my friend missed most was having no one to read her children's reports to over the phone. 'She was the only one apart from myself who had any real interest in them, who would shriek with delight if they were good, and feel livid with the teachers if they were bad. There is no one to share both the joys and the pains with.'

Sometimes you can get obsessed by your own loneliness, crying not only because of the loss of affection for the person who has died, but also through letting your mind roam over how unhappy you will be when other people, people who are now perfectly healthy, die in the future as well. It is as if one torments oneself by practising in fantasy how it might be if everyone one loved died, and only oneself were left.

Some partners miss particularly the comfort of physical closeness. One widow, commenting on her loneliness, said: 'No one touches me any more. Not just sexually, but simply as another human being.' And in *The Empty Bed*, Susan Wallbank quoted a widow as saying:

> Over the past nine years I have found the loss of cuddling, kissing, hard to bear ... leave alone making love. It sometimes seems so incredible that all my life, having enjoyed the warmth of physical contact, with first my parents, and then Bob, I am now isolated in some refrigerator of iron-grey loneliness. It is akin to solitary confinement.

But for all these griefs – for the lost past, the lost future, the companionship, the sex, the potential, the promise, one's own hopes and dreams – what does it feel like when you suffer? And what is the suffering, exactly? It is usually described as having a life of its own, unconnected with the person who has died.

Grief sometimes seems to exist not because of the other person, but instead of them.

> Grief fills the room up of my absent child,
> Lies in his bed, walks up and down with me,
> Puts on his pretty looks, repeats his words,
> Remembers me of all his gracious parts,
> Stuffs out his vacant garments with his form . . .
>
> (William Shakespeare, *King John*)

So many people describe grief as a thing, something that can 'hit you'. So one minute you can be being perfectly normal and then suddenly, wham – this terrible feeling overcomes you. Despite the fact that he has inner resources, and the knowledge that people get over these things, C. S. Lewis wrote: 'Then comes a sudden jab of red-hot memory and all this "commonsense" vanishes like an ant in the mouth of a furnace . . . ' He describes the sickening moment, so utterly familiar to anyone who opens their eyes and experiences, for a moment, the feeling of waking before reality dawns: 'I hear a clock strike and some quality it always had before has gone out of the sound. What's wrong with the world to make it so flat, shabby, worn-out looking? Then I remember.'

And then, just as he starts to feel he's getting himself sorted out, and has got something organized for himself: 'Unfortunately, it can't be carried out. Tonight all the hells of young grief have opened again; the mad words, the bitter resentment, the fluttering in the stomach, the nightmare unreality, the wallowed-in tears. For in grief nothing "stays put".'

Helen Osborne said: 'Grief is the most complicated thing. You might be driving, you think you're perfectly all right, and then you have to stop the car because you can't see for tears. You long to be home so you can go upstairs and be on your own. You feel like a child. I've started having Horlicks at night.'

C. S. Lewis also talks of the gluey, almost self-indulgent quality of grief. 'On the rebound one passes into tears and pathos. Maudlin tears. I almost prefer the moments of agony. These are at least clean and honest. But the bath of self-pity, the wallow, the loathsome sticky-sweet pleasure of indulging it – that disgusts me.'

A bereaved person can find tears everywhere. He can find grief in hearing of another death – or a birth; he can find grief in the comforting cuddle of a friend – or when another friend fails to return a call; he can find grief in a young child's smile, simply because it seems so full of innocence of what lies ahead – or he can find grief in a young child's tears; he can find grief in a family celebration because the dead person isn't there to share it; he can find grief in pleasure and grief in sadness.

As Rebecca Abrams wrote, nine months after her stepfather's death:

> Yet another day spent wandering around in tears. When is this depression going to lift? It is so exhausting this feeling of lethargic misery. I feel isolated and lonely the whole time. I still haven't accepted that he is dead. I still imagine he is alive. I hate him and Dad for having died. Five days in every seven I am depressed. I feel lonely and miserable and depressed . . . A movie can spark off misery – even a movie designed to cheer one up.

In *Other People*, her diaries from 1963 to 1966, Frances Partridge wrote, after the death of her husband:

> The sky is pure blue and the sun has developed a midsummer strength. I am lying on my bed at 4 pm trying to fight off despair. I'm not sure that I *can* stand much more of this. I have no libido to put into anything. It suddenly seems to me an act of insane folly to try to go on; it strikes me as illogical, irrational, even uncharacteristic behaviour, which I'm unable to justify and feel positively apologetic for. I am like a trailer that has broken loose and is rattling down hill out of control.

In an earlier diary, *Hanging On*, she wrote:

Sometimes I imagine I have been undergoing a long, long surgical operation or series of operations. 'Yes, I'm afraid we must remove one arm, one leg, part of your side. Yes, the whole amputation will be done at one go but there will be a long subsequent stage of minor operations sealing off nerves and arteries, grafting new skin, cauterizations. Painful? Yes, very, I'm afraid, but nothing can be done about it; you must just hold tight to this bar when the pain gets unbearable, bite on the bullet.

'Prognosis? Well, your life will be limited, of course, but it will be life of a sort.'

A feeble attempt at 'fighting back' last night was not a great success.

It is the discovery of one's own vulnerability that is so very frightening. Anything can set you off. As someone who is basically all to pieces or totally in control, I've never understood it when people describe themselves as having 'tears that are never far away'. And yet after my father died, tears seemed to be glittering behind the eyes, all the time, just waiting for a trigger, any trigger . . . a kitten, a stray dog, a happy family, an unhappy family, an item about an adopted child finding her real mother, or a father losing his son in an accident . . . and then the feeling of sadness would get more intense and burst out at all kinds of times, in the stillness of a church service, at a film, over a flash of memory. And there was a temporary relief in crying, although it often wasn't actually about my father. I would seek out things to make me cry.

How healing is crying? It's fashionable to attach enormous importance to the expulsion of salty water from the eyes. And yet not everyone cries. And, indeed, there are actually those who don't cry and who *don't* fulfil the counsellors' prophecies that they will become wizened old walnuts of illness and repression. Even so, there is a cruel current school of thought that argues that if you don't cry, something dreadful will happen to you. 'Healing tears' they are called. 'Have a good cry then everything will be all right.' Certainly a good cry can make everything temporarily all right, but tears are not an end in themselves. After all, some people, as we'll see later, get stuck in their grief, and just go on crying and crying till they die. So much for the healing power of tears.

Perhaps it is the type of tears that is important. That's another theory. One widow was quoted as saying that for six months she'd 'cried, but not really cried, if you understand what I mean . . . I cried on the surface, but not properly crying, and I sort of survived and survived and survived, and it was a week in June . . . I completely went to pieces . . . I couldn't stop crying . . . It was almost as if the protective layer was coming off.'

According to some psychologists, there are different types of crying: shallow weeping and deep weeping. Shallow weeping is the stuff to avoid, they say, because it means there's constant tension in the body, which results in a lasting sense of grief. It is not the frequency of the grief, it's argued, but the depth. In other words, quality crying.

We are the only species that cries, and much is made of it all. But where does crying get us, except a temporary respite from pain? Is crying any more than an emotional aspirin? I talk with more experience than most because I cry buckets at least three times a week, and have to report, to those who find it difficult, that, rather like a stiff drink, it doesn't always offer more than short-term relief. For me anyway. And I've tried all varieties, shallow and deep. I mention this only to reassure those poor folk who find it difficult to squeeze a drop from their eyes and torment themselves with guilt and anguish about the whole business, worrying that their repression will cause them an early death.

'My father has always cried easily: he cried when dogs and cats died; he cried when he left my sister at her boarding-school; he cried waving goodbye from under our chestnut tree the day I went off to university,' wrote Blake Morrison in *And When Did You Last See Your Father?*

So why had he taught me to be brave and hold it in? Why have I never been able to cry? Why can't I cry for him? Even now, shaking myself loose of the dog and at once coming across a photo of my father from a year ago – tanned, happy, arms round his grandchildren on the beach – even now the tears won't come.

It is not essential to cry. Grief can go on underground. It may leave a bitter taste in the mouth, but unless you have got stuck in grieving – which is possible whether you cry or not – the integration, if that is the right word, of the feelings after a bereavement into your life is just as likely. Older people, for example, according to Dr Colin Murray Parkes, may generally experience less extreme outbursts of despair and rage, and even sudden bereavement may seem less devastating in its overall consequences, while young people may find it harder to grieve – in other words to cry and give in to the sad feelings of loss – partly because they are often burdened too young with big responsibilities that they're not ready for.

It isn't the tears that are important, but the feelings, I think. It is easy to cry without focused feeling, just out of a general sense of misery; but one genuine authentic feeling is worth a million tears. And identifying and articulating that feeling, even to yourself, gives you some kind of comfort, for it is a kind of control. It is something that belongs to *you*. And when you are grieving and feel you have nothing, every little bit counts; every bit of self, every feeling, be it good or bad, is something to grab at. Recognize it, define it, capture it in a net and pin it down on a board; then it becomes something, instead of an amorphous, loathsome emotion floating free and foggy in the air.

> Give sorrow words: the grief that does not speak
> Whispers the o'er-fraught heart, and bids it break.
> (William Shakespeare, *Macbeth*)

Evelyn Waugh felt that words were a kind of lubricant for grief, though he rightly argued that they didn't make the suffer-

ing any less great. In *Work Suspended* he wrote about how his
hero's tears finally came after he visited his dead painter father's
studio.

> Now the words came; I began, in my mind, to lament my
> father, addressing, as it were, funeral orations to my own
> literary memories, and sorrow, dammed and canalized,
> flowed fast.
>
> For the civilized man there are none of those swift transi-
> tions of joy and pain which possess the savage; words form
> slowly like pus about his hurts; there are no clean wounds
> for him; first a numbness, then a long festering, then a scar
> ever ready to re-open. Not until they have assumed the
> livery of the defence can his emotions pass through the
> lines; sometimes they come massed in a wooden horse,
> sometimes as single spies, but there is always a Fifth
> Column among the garrison ready to receive them. Sabo-
> tage behind the lines, a blind raised and lowered at a lighted
> window, a wire cut, a bolt loosened, a file disordered – that
> is how the civilized man is undone.

But it is not so much how we become undone that interests
the bereaved person. It is how soon they can become done up
again. How long does this agony last? When will it go away? It
really is impossible to say. When it comes to feeling despairing
and grief-stricken, it's true that most people fall into the slough
of despond and slowly crawl out the other side. But there are
other options. One is to sink into it, to wish yourself dead, and
lack the energy to pull yourself slowly together to start living
again. Suicides after someone close has died are not common,
but they do happen; there is apparently some truth in the
theory that after the death of a partner, the chances of
the surviving partner lasting long aren't as great as in those
people who have not been closely bereaved. It's a rare bereaved person who hasn't at least considered the pleasures
of death after a close loved one has died. One widow wanted to
dig up the grave and just climb in with her husband. And this

teenager, who had a miscarriage, spoke for people bereaved in all kinds of other ways.

> I was so depressed I couldn't even sleep. I missed my baby so much I wanted to be with her, so I took an overdose of paracetamol, but a friend found me and took me to hospital where I saw a psychiatrist who was very nice. But I still can't cope with my feelings. I just bottle them up. I can't snap out of this depression and it seems to get worse every day. I feel everyone is against me because of my mood swings. I blame myself so much thinking that I might have been able to have prevented it, like, what if I didn't go out that day, would I have still carried it? I ask myself every question, over and over again, torturing myself. It has been five months since the miscarriage but only seems five days. Everyone tells me I am still young but it doesn't matter. I am trying to find the strength to carry on, but it is difficult, especially when you've lost a baby that you thought was yours to keep and not let anyone take it away from you as it was a part of you. A part of me is lost with my baby, a part of me that I may never find. My heart is broken and I'm trying to find the missing piece . . .

Life seems to have no meaning any more. Sometimes it gets so bad that grief actually dries up altogether, leaving the bereaved person with a terrible sense of nothingness, utter bleakness. Tom Stoppard, in *Rosencrantz and Guildenstern are Dead*, wrote: 'Death isn't romantic . . . death is not anything . . . death is . . . not. It's the absence of presence, nothing more . . . a gap you can't see, and when the wind blows through it makes no sound.' And Mary Stott wrote in the *Guardian* of the utter pointlessness she felt after her husband died:

> At this stage, Death is the friend, Life is the enemy. It seemed to me at this time that being alive was just a habit, and a habit that had now become very disagreeable. Now I had been jolted out of the normal view that it is obviously

better to be alive than dead, it seemed a ludicrous proposition. What was so wonderful about being alive? Sixty years of life had habituated me to eating at certain times, washing, dressing, going to work, doing this and that but *what for*? Why spend another ten or twenty years doing all these things just for the sake of being alive? There were, it is true, fleeting moments of pleasure but there was nothing, *nothing*, that made the future look anything but a dreary, meaningless trudge. The concept of life as a duty, in the abstract, struck me as monstrous.

After her partner, Mel Calman, died, the novelist Deborah Moggach shared similar feelings of futility. 'Grief is a foreign country,' she wrote.

One crosses the border and there is no going back. I remember, in the past few days, looking in my diary and seeing appointments written in it. Appointments for what? For who? *Me*. I went into a hardware shop to buy a corkscrew and stood beside a stand full of gadgets. They were all for pitifully silly things. I thought: Mel has died and somebody has actually thought of inventing something to cut pizza edges and take the stones out of cherries. Why? One feels frail and elderly, afraid of honking cars and of people shouting in the street. One dreads official letters – bank letters, parking summonses – because they seem so impossibly difficult.

In her diaries, Frances Partridge wrote after her husband's death:

I hate doing my life sentence and would gladly abandon it for ever – would like to lay down my life as one drops a handkerchief. Death is always in my thoughts now, and tears make a high water mark in the inside of my head. Why live unloved, unwarmed (who cares if I do or not?) with no one to laugh with and share my preoccupations? Why haul and heave to pull my courage up from the bottom of the well it has dropped into? Since one must fix on some landmark ahead, I'm going to try to think of going to Spain in just over a month's time, as a prisoner thinks of the next visit he's allowed. My misery is a dreadful acid which dissolves the mental processes, obliterates the memory and slows up the responses – an attempt to commit suicide on the part of the brain.

Often survivors want to die, but can't because others depend on them. The husband of Rachel Nickell, who was murdered on Wimbledon Common, was quoted as saying:

> Many times I wish I was dead but I can't be dead because I can't leave my son on his own. He's always going to need me and in a way it's a life sentence. I can't even be miserable. I can't afford to be bitter. I can't walk around all day screaming and shouting and swearing and wanting to kill people.

And a woman who had just had a miscarriage said: 'People say: "Don't be sad, for you're only young and there's so much more life to live." But how strange I feel as I lie here at night. The tomorrows seem already to have gone.'

Some people find these feelings gradually diminish in intensity and overwhelm them less often. But there are some who like to linger in the valley of death. They don't want to stop being unhappy, and they won't. Unhappiness is the last vestige of contact they have with the dead person; as long as they hang on feeling miserable, they are still connected. Being miserable for the rest of your life over a death is one way of not letting the loved one go. We wait, like dumb dogs for a master that has gone away never to return, pining at the door, waiting, listening, tensing for every movement. Was that rustle his step on the drive? . . . A key in the door? Friends can try to drag us away, but doggedly we remain rooted to the spot. (And why not? Perhaps this state of waiting is more comfortable than facing the pain of realization that the loved one has gone for ever.)

Talking in the *Independent* to Danny Danziger about his aunt and her son Jack, who died on a training session in an aeroplane, Brian Glover said:

He was buried in Barnsley, our Jack, I can remember the funeral. And every day of her life, and she only died about three or four years ago, Aunt Dorrie went to that cemetery, and they even gave her keys so she could go in on her own. She never went away on holiday, so she could go to the cemetery. It ruined her life. His death took everything fun out of that house and her daughter was never really cared for after that. The house became a shrine to Jack, and on the walls were photographs of the crew who also died in the plane.

Harry Corbett's widow said in the *Daily Mail* that she will never recover from Harry's death and, more interestingly, that she doesn't much want to anyway.

Friends tell me that what I need is a good weep. That I should weep Harry out. But I don't want to get shot of Harry Corbett. I don't want to cry him out. He was a lovely, loving man. He put me on a pedestal and I put him on one. I don't want to forget him.

And in Lawrence Whistler's account of his wife's life and death, he wrote:

A friend assured me in his letter that though I could not see beyond the suffering I should in time come through it. I laughed, that his consolation should be so unconsoling; for I wanted nothing better than to live always in the immediacy of loss. In the sharpness of it I felt near to her. The worst was the best. What was unendurable was precisely the idea of 'coming through' . . . Clarity was what I longed for now. If she faded altogether, I thought, that would be the real goodbye; whereas grieving was only loving in another key.

It is sometimes easier to dog-paddle in the gloom than strike out for the shore. Perhaps it is impossible to strike out for the shore. And anyway, it is rarely a bereaved person's choice. If they are the sort of people who stay trapped in their grief, we should respect their feelings. Certainly people yelling: 'Get a move on!' won't help. Susan Hill beautifully described the agonizing sense of loneliness suffered by Dora, beside herself with grief over the death of her son, Ben. Her daughter, Alice, comes up to her and harangues her when she's crying.

> 'Stop that! Stop that, mother, how do you think we can bear to hear you, crying and crying, and complaining? Don't you think we feel, too? Don't you think all of us feel, but what good are you doing? What help is it? . . . It does no good, does it? Will it alter things? Will it bring him back? Haven't you any dignity, any pride in yourself . . . *What good will it do?*'

> Dora Bryce did not answer, only moved nearer the fire, trapped in the vicious circle of her own misery and resentment. She thought, now my daughter is turning against me, and what have I left? . . .

People around bereaved people can get impatient far too soon. Friends were forever recommending I saw a psychiatrist, not understanding that my depression was due to the tremendous hard work that was going on actually acknowledging that my father was dead. They may have seen me as stuck in depression, but I knew that though I appeared to be sinking, under the muddy water I was trying out all kinds of cunning leg-movements to propel me to the shore.

Or was I trying out cunning leg-movements? To be honest it felt much more as if bereavement were doing it for me, and that I was reacting to some kind of force over which I had no control. After a baby is born, it doesn't beaver away to grow up, to stand, to walk; it is something that happens spontaneously in its body. Assimilating the facts and feelings around a bereavement, the process is much the same. The only power we have lies in our own personalities, and whether we are the sort of people who resist strong feelings, are barely but just able to cope with them, ride the waves like champion surfers, or are drowned by them.

Some people are dominated by the tyranny of tears; but others would be hard pressed to get through so much as a Kleenex Handipak. There are plenty of other ways, however, for them to react after a death.

7. . . . And Other Responses

My father's death meant a very great deal to me. He had told me that
we should not mourn when he died. As far as he was concerned you
could throw the body away . . . When I came back to California after
the funeral I kept thinking about him and I thought, in my head he's
still there. He is always there, he won't go away; and so it is now . . .
He was seventy-six when he died. He'd had a very full life. He had
five children who were still there, grandchildren, and I thought, it
was a rich life; we shouldn't mourn for him, we should be pleased,
actually. (David Hockney, who sees death as 'not totally tragic . . .
maybe it's just another adventure', talking about his father's death)

Although authors and psychologists have tried to capture the
feelings of bereavement, pinning down the stages as clearly as
diagrams of a developing child in the womb, any reactions that
don't fit neatly into the grief 'pattern' are usually quietly
dropped. The truth, however, is that feelings after a bereavement vary enormously; one woman, after her mother had
died, rang me up, asked if I would go over and split a bottle
of champagne, and added: 'When she's buried we can go and
dance on her grave.' But even the spouses of the most loathed
partners or children of the most hated parents are rarely so
honest, since it is in their own interests to perceive death as
awful and sad; otherwise not only might people condemn
them for not caring, but the bereaved might also miss out on the
highly seductive sympathy that they all should get, like some
kind of birthday present, after a death. Unfortunately, being
dishonest about the reaction to a death performs no service to
others: the dead person won't know anyway, the bereaved
person feels lonely, lying to themselves about some of their
reactions, and the only result is that the myth about how it
is 'normal' to behave and feel after a bereavement is simply
perpetuated, making it all the more difficult for others when

82

they, too, act, or feel, in what is perceived as a 'strange' way after a loss.

What about the reaction of Jim Davidson, the comedian, when his mother died of lung cancer after being in a coma? He was too upset to cry. 'I didn't have any tears left. I gave her a kiss goodbye when she was in a coma, went home and didn't know what to do with myself. I put on a really sad episode of *Star Trek* and watched that.'

When Toby Young's mother died, he found his feelings at odds with those who felt he 'ought' to feel. In the *Mail on Sunday* he wrote:

I bridle at the thought that there's a right and wrong way to respond to things like this, that my reaction to my mother's death was emotionally incorrect. If I had to defend myself, I'd say that death is a truly terrible thing and that any ritual or technique that helps you accept it only does so by disguising its true nature. Not thinking about it is preferable to pretending it's something else, something that can be 'coped with'.

Others, too, have not found that wailing and gnashing of teeth are at all appropriate. And why should they? I doubt if I have shed a tear after my mother's death, and even my father's death left me only baffled, furious and shocked, but not, confusingly, grief-stricken – at least, not about him.

The first group who step outside the bereaving, grieving norm are the no-fussers. Death's quite normal, we had a good time while it lasted, he or she would not have wanted me to be unhappy, so I shall get on with life as usual. Sensible, says society. (But, golly, how very unnatural, they whisper among themselves!) And yet Ursula Bowlby, writing about the death of her husband, the psychologist John Bowlby, said:

Instead of being shattered I felt suddenly comforted. He seemed secure in my heart and I knew I would carry him about with me for the rest of my life. I have this sense of

continuous companionship. I am never lonely. I can't understand the 'how' or 'why' but as a believer I accept it as a
wonderful gift from God. And I know it will last, because
although I didn't expect it, I recognize it. My greatly loved
mother died twelve years ago, aged eighty-eight, and the
same thing happened then. I had spent my life dreading
losing her, yet when she died I felt her safe in my heart, and
free – free from the disabilities of old age. She is still in my
heart. The two people I most dreaded losing are not lost to
me.

The astrologer Patric Walker lost his mother and closest friend
in a car crash, but still didn't feel too much pain.

I do not grieve for the people I've lost. I will not grieve.
Time was, they were, we were. It will always remain beautiful. You may physically never see them again, but your love
for them isn't diminished. It's not something to wail over.
But it's rather nice now. What about the people who love
you and want you and need you now? I don't know why we
haven't been educated – and again, this probably goes back
to losing my mother – that we have a life span. If you're
going to go, you're going to go. That's all there is. There
isn't any more.

When my widower friend was looking through the papers he
saw a picture in a colour supplement that moved him greatly.

It was by Lucien Freud. It showed a naked couple in bed.
She was sleeping on her side, one foot resting on his thigh;
he was lying on his back with one arm resting against her
back. They have, from their relaxed poses, just finished
making love. It took me back to us, how often we had lain
in exactly that situation, relaxed and deeply happy with
each other. It is the sort of picture that had you never
experienced what it showed might have tormented you
beyond endurance, but as we were fortunate it cheered me
up a bit with good memories.

Colin Murray Parkes quoted a widow who declared that she could feel her husband guiding her.

> It is not a sense of his presence, he is here inside me. That's why I am happy all the time. As if two people were one . . . although I am alone we are, sort of, together if you see what I mean . . . I don't think I have the willpower to carry on on my own, so he must be.

The wretched thing about all this is that if you do grieve, people are nagging at you to cheer up; but if you don't grieve people are nagging at you to grieve. They are comfortable with some grief, but not too much. They are comfortable with some good cheer – but again, not too much. But society has a ridiculous idea about what is 'correct'. If you let not a tear descend your cheek you're cold and psychotic; if you cry and cry for years, heads are shaken, and your friends may even start shouting at you to pull yourself together. If you feel as Pauline Johnston, the widow of broadcaster Brian Johnston, described in the *Daily Mail* after his death, coming to terms with it in a quietly sad and joyful way, other people will insist on describing how you *should* or *will* experience the loss.

> I've had such a wonderful marriage for forty-five years to a wonderful man. We had five children, seven grandchildren. I feel fulfilled. Why should I crack up? Brian wouldn't want me to do that. It wasn't his way. People say 'Oh, you'll have good days and bad days, you'll get fits of depression'. But I haven't had them yet. Brian did everything he wanted to and he went out right at the top. I am sad inside, but I keep it to myself. I'm just so grateful for what we had.

The 'no fuss' approach to death is difficult enough for other people to come to terms with, and often, as we've seen, makes the no-fussers themselves feel strangely guilty and marginalized. Even more difficult for bereaved people to cope with is lack of feelings altogether. Death just seems no big deal. Perhaps we never had any strong feelings about the person who died – most of those tearful hangers-on at funerals are usually crying for something quite other than the actual person's death – or perhaps we had got over our grief before the person died, because they were emotionally unavailable to us from an early age.

Sally St Clair wrote, in a story in *Death of a Mother*:

At the funeral, the vicar, whom I didn't know at all, said she was a saint. He said she was a wonderful mother and a wonderful wife who had always had time to help other people. He said she would be missed by many people. Well, I miss her. I miss her because she was my mother. Apart from that, there is nothing for me to miss: I never knew who she was, and so what I will always miss – for ever – is the chance to find out. And I think that she died to make sure she didn't ever have to find out.

Lack of feelings may also be experienced when a person dies after suffering from a drawn-out illness, and those around have had time to come to terms with the sadness long before their hearts stopped beating.

In these cases you can go through the death in your mind, rehearse it, and experience some of the bereavement feelings before they actually happen. This is called 'anticipatory grieving'. Psychiatrist Professor Brice Pitt found that the worst effects of bereavement are avoidable by this type of grieving.

It has been found that the women who grieve in advance for the womb or breast they have to lose cope much better afterwards than those who close their minds to the impending loss until it has actually happened. The same technique can be applied where the death of a loved one, say from cancer or motor neurone disease, is predictable.

And the classic case of anticipatory grieving comes from the Bible (2 Samuel 12: 17–23), in which King David mourned his son's death in advance.

The elders of his house arose and went to him, to raise

him up from the earth: but he would not, neither did he eat bread with them.

And it came to pass on the seventh day, that the child died. And the servants of David feared to tell him that the child was dead: for they said, Behold, while the child was yet alive, we spake unto him, and he would not hearken unto our voice: how will he then vex himself, if we tell him that the child is dead?

But when David saw that his servants whispered, David perceived that the child was dead: therefore David said unto his servants, Is the child dead: And they said, He is dead.

Then David arose from the earth, and washed and anointed himself and changed his apparel and came into the house of the Lord and worshipped: then he came to his own house: and when he required, they set bread before him, and he did eat.

Then said his servants unto him, What thing is this that thou has done? Thou didst fast and weep for the child while it was alive: but when the child was dead, thou didst rise and eat bread. [Wonderful to read of the social pressure on David to grieve 'properly' even thousands of years ago!] And he said, While the child was yet alive, I fasted and wept: for I said, Who can tell whether God will be gracious to me, that the child may live? But now he is dead, wherefore should I fast? Can I bring him back again? I shall go to him, but he shall not return to me.

Not only did King David have the advantage of anticipatory grieving, he also had the strong faith that he would meet his son again one day. Older people may feel more resigned about death, too, because they may have suffered so many more bereavements than a younger person. It would not be fair to say they have become hardened; it is more that they have learned to accept death as a part of life.

Some people don't grieve while they're awake but their grief works through them in unspeakable dreams. These may not just be the kind of dreams that linger for an hour or two after the dreamer has woken up; they are dreams that can haunt for weeks, clouding the brain with horror as if the devil has stirred it with a spoon. They were the sort experienced by Toby Young after his mother's death.

I didn't really grieve, not in any conventional sense. I cried whenever I thought of her, but when I wasn't thinking about her it didn't seem to affect me. I amazed myself by being able to get on with my life perfectly easily. People told me I was in denial, repressing my grief. One man, someone I scarcely knew, told me he thought it was wrong the way I was carrying on as normal, that I should be breaking down or staring into space or . . . well, whatever it is people do when their mothers die.

Oddly enough, I didn't feel particularly guilty or bad about not grieving. On the face of it, the reason people were shocked was because it made me seem rather heartless and cold. But I wasn't in any doubt about how much I loved my mother, there just didn't seem much point in thinking about the fact that I'd never see her again . . . I was presented with all the usual reasons for grieving: if you don't do it now you'll only have to do it later; it's best to get it out of your system; it helps the healing process. But this apparent concern for my welfare, giving me all sorts of selfish reasons to grieve, was at odds with the disapproval they obviously felt. They just thought I ought to be grieving.

The fact that I was expected to be grief-stricken in public made me even less inclined to be so. I wasn't going to start grieving just because it was the socially acceptable thing to do; I wasn't going to alter my behaviour just to meet with other people's approval. But privately, in my dream life, things were going haywire. Dreams about my mother were not like other dreams in that she would be so much more real than people usually are. She wasn't in colour, and I couldn't smell her, but her presence was over-whelming. I was literally able to touch her. I used to wake up sobbing uncontrollably, feeling closer to her than I ever had in life.

After the article was published in which these thoughts ap-peared, several readers wrote in to confirm their relief at reading the expression of such feelings. 'It seems that your response to your mother's death was very close to my own – and, I suspect, many others. Whilst I never had any problem in justifying my feelings or response to either myself or anybody else, it was very pleasing to feel that they were in no way "unique" or "suspect",' wrote one. And another: 'I don't feel grief-stricken and people around me seem to think that this isn't normal.'

There are often feelings of understandable relief. When some-one has been a pain in the neck all their life, why not be suffused with delight when they die? When someone has made you miser-able, by all means go out and rejoice. When someone has suf-fered an agonizing illness, you may be a little sad when they die, but if you have an ounce of humanity in you, you will feel waves of relief for both your sakes. In *How We Die*, Sherwin B. Nuland wrote of the feelings of a great friend of his, Janet, when her husband, Phil, died from Alzheimer's disease.

I was glad. I know it sounds terrible to say that, but I was happy he was relieved of that degrading sickness. I knew he never suffered, and I knew he had no idea what was happening to him, and I was grateful for that. It was a blessing – it was the only thing that kept me going, all of those months and years. But it was a horrible thing to watch happening to someone I loved so much.

When someone she had befriended at the London Lighthouse died of AIDS, Maria Cantacuzino had mixed feelings on his death.

It would have been a lie to say that I did not feel a hint of relief at Kim's death – not only because I did not have to make those long and difficult visits any more but also because the release that he had so been waiting for had finally come. But when the news was broken to me on the phone I was surprised to find my eyes filling with tears.

Death is known as the last taboo. But the taboo that is even greater is happiness or relief at death. It is just 'not on'. People do not want to hear it. I could talk to very few people about my feelings after my mother's death. I would buttonhole them trying to tell them how she had wanted to die, how she had tried to commit suicide but had died of cancer, how she had said 'Thank you' when I told her I had asked the doctor to give her a fatal injection and that she would die at last, how I felt a burden lift from my shoulders when she died – and my listeners would turn away in horror. 'I don't want to hear it,' said one, and others, who deliberately *didn't* hear what I was saying, simply said, 'You must feel terribly sad,' and pressed my hand, their eyes welling with tears.

In *A Special Scar*, Alison Wertheimer quotes a girl whose sister committed suicide.

Almost from the day it happened I felt a sense of relief. Often I wasn't sure who this was for – her or me? Perhaps it was for both of us. Even so I can still find it hard to admit sometimes that I feel glad I don't have to worry about her any more; her problems and crises don't interrupt my life. But we're not supposed to be glad when someone dies.

In a story in *Death of a Mother* Leland Bardwell wrote:

Two days before she died my father got a real nurse. Two real nurses. Night nurse and day nurse. I got a sore throat. I also got a new grey coat. I was glad she was dead.

My sister and my father cried. In the church, that was. We had coffee in the silver coffee-pot. It tasted good. It was a cold February day. I felt light as a jenny-wren.

People who have had entirely happy marriages may often find, even in the middle of feeling unhappy, a weird sense of freedom when their partner dies, a feeling of release from being conjoined to another person. They are often suddenly aware of how much their own personality was buried or enmeshed with the other's. There is a feeling of emancipation, a longing to shout: 'Free at last!' that can exist simultaneously alongside the grief. And many is the man who suddenly finds that his wife has been keeping the joys of cooking from him for years, or the woman who delights in suddenly taking charge of everything and thrills, at last, to be in the driving seat in the car.

In another story from *Death of a Mother*, Suzanne Bosworth wrote:

> In the last year I have sensed her presence in and around me like some malevolent miasma, pouring into my dreams, suffocating my spirit and threatening to engulf and annihilate me. How dare I finally explode the secrecy?! How dare I start to feel happy, confident, loved, worthwhile?! How dare I escape her stronghold?!

There is also straightforward relief from a dreadful burden, here described by a child as yet unhampered by society's expectations of what she 'should' say. Jill Krementz quotes a young girl who puts her feelings quite frankly:

> In a way I'm glad that my mother died when she did because she was always going to be an invalid. As it is, my childhood was shot. I mean, I could never go away to summer camp. Who was going to take care of my mother? I was very, very thin because in the morning I would get up and make my mother breakfast. God, I was only nine. I had to make myself breakfast too but I usually didn't bother because then I'd be late for school. Then I used to rush home at noon, make my mother lunch and rush back to school. In the evening my aunt would make dinner so I'd go over to her place, eat and then bring dinner for my

mother. She was a complete invalid. She couldn't do any-thing for herself. So I mean if she were still alive, what would we have done with her? I would have had to spend the rest of my life taking care of her.

If adults' reaction to death is territory uncharted enough, children's reactions are even more of a mystery. Often they can grieve and cry along so-called 'normal' lines, and naturally should be encouraged to do so rather than artificially cheered up by inappropriate trips to zoos and McDonald's. In fact it seems that children tend to recover more quickly than adults from even the worst disasters, but only if they are allowed to do it their way, and feel no inhibitions about behaving peculiarly or sadly if they wish.

In the cases of the death of a parent or, particularly, a sibling, a child can, if not handled very gently, easily deny that he feels anything. As it really is highly unlikely that this is the case, it may be a time for an adult to prompt feelings of abandonment, sadness, and fear, lest the children's feelings do continue into adult life. Just because a child plays happily and says nothing doesn't mean necessarily that he has got over a death remarkably quickly. It's what we want to be the case, but almost certainly it's not what's going on. This child could, of course, just not be feeling anything – or he could be denying his feelings. It's ex-tremely difficult to know, but children, who may be emotionally naïve, should be given the opportunity to express their feelings, although obviously not nagged into doing so. Jill Kre-mentz quotes a child talking, after her mother had died:

I blocked it out of my head. I didn't want to think about it. I wanted to get on with my life. The next day I was fine and I was laughing and playing with my cousins. And when I got back to school I acted the same way I did before. I just felt a lot better by not thinking about it.

Some children become destructive after a death. One com-pletely ruined his room, pulling down all the posters on the walls and cutting up his sheets. Others may start lying or stealing. Children, because they tend to think they are the centre of the universe, may be convinced that they were responsible for the death. If a child behaves particularly badly, too, it's usually a sign of anger about the death, and remarks like: 'How can you behave so badly when you know we're all so upset about X's death?' are exceptionally cruel. The child's bad behaviour is only a sign that he, too, is upset.

Finding it difficult to articulate their feelings and sometimes feeling too overwhelmed to cry, children can express their sadness in pictures or drawings, story-telling or the type of play they indulge in. They can also get withdrawn, sulky, bad-tempered and depressed, and none of these feelings, if grief-related, should be punished or criticized.

Some bereavement counsellors remark that children don't grieve in the same way as adults, but to say this implies that there is a 'way' that adults grieve, when in fact there is an infinity of ways. Perhaps it would be truer to say that the ways that children grieve are often even less familiar to us than the odd ways adults grieve. Little could be odder than the poor ten-year-old Bob Monkhouse, who suffered dreadfully when his beloved grand-father, the only person who appears to have loved him at all, died.

The effect of his death on me was profound. I lost the ability to speak and remained more or less silent for just over three months. It was possible for me to make a noise with my vocal cords, but it was uncontrollable and unintelli-gible and it frightened me to hear myself. During my tenth birthday party I made a great effort to use my tongue and lips to produce a little speech of thanks but it was as if they were paralysed and I ran upstairs in tears. Schoolwork was difficult, and unkind boys made fun of me. When I began to talk again, it was with a stutter that affected all words beginning with vowels. Even today, the same stam-mer can return if I am severely shocked.

Adults are less commonly affected by this kind of extreme shock. They are more likely to be tormented by shameful thoughts that they often feel they could never confide in anyone else for fear of being thought callous. One quite common reaction is the feeling of 'Phew! There but for the grace of God go I.' Two writers described the same feeling very differently. Tolstoy, never one to shrink from describing emotions painfully accurately, wrote in *The Death of Ivan Ilyich*:

> Besides the reflections upon the transfers and possible changes in the department likely to result from Ivan Ilyich's decease, the mere fact of the death of an intimate associate aroused, as is usual, in all who heard of it a complacent feeling that 'it is he who is dead, and not I. Now he had to go and die but I manage things better – I am alive,' each of them thought or felt.

In *The Rummy Affair of Old Biffy*, P. G. Wodehouse described Biffy's feelings of relief on escaping from his engagement to Honoria Glossop, daughter of the famous brain doctor, Sir Roderick:

> I should imagine a fellow would feel much the same if he happened to be strolling through the jungle with a boyhood chum and met a tigress or a jaguar, or what not, and managed to shin up a tree and looked down and saw the friend of his youth vanishing into the undergrowth in the animal's slavering jaws. A sort of profound, prayerful relief, if you know what I mean, blended at the same time with a pang of pity.

P. G. Wodehouse? What's he doing here? It may seem inappropriate for his name to be mentioned in a book about bereavement, but humour, particularly gallows humour, is another extremely common reaction to death. In the first few days or weeks after a death, bereaved people may be appalled to find how much they are laughing. Laughing like drains. Screaming with laughter. The shock of a death makes everything vivid, and we often feel much more aware of our emotions than we normally do, feel strangely present in a world in which we normally just act like robots. Our senses may become acute, and since laughter and tears are good bedfellows, it's not surprising that a certain hilarity often prevails, particularly during the days of shock, around the funeral.

When my father died our family spent much of the following day in hysterics. Crying, yes, but shrieking with laughter as well. When a kind man popped in to sympathize and, on learning that my father had engraved some glass in his time, murmured: 'Yes, yes, grave-englassing, very interesting,' some of us had to leave the room to stifle our howls of laughter. When the undertaker turned to my stepmother and, getting out his clipboard, announced: ''ubby?' to her, we imitated him later to each other and told the story for days afterwards. What my dignified and classy father would have thought being referred to as ''ubby' we could not imagine, but we knew that he would laugh as well.

When the poet George Barker died, his widow, Elspeth, commented on the

moments of inadvertent mirth. There was the fund-raising letter from the Samaritans which arrived the day after George's death – 'Dear Mr Barker, Have you ever felt you couldn't last one more day?' – then the early-morning call from the undertaker, intercepted by my daughter. 'Sorry to disturb you. We just wanted to know if you'd like your dad's grave dug extra deep? So your mum can go in, too.'

A daughter said that when they opened their mother's Christmas present to her grandchildren after she had died they discovered that her young sons had been given the most dreadful noisy battery-operated guns. 'When I laughingly reported to friends that my mother must have known she would not be alive at Christmas to be driven mad by the noise, they looked shocked.'

And Rebecca Abrams wrote that when the vicar called her father Philip Abrahams – to which in life he had always responded: 'No H. A-B-R-A-M-S' – she and her brother thought her

dad would rise from his coffin to say 'No H. A-B-R-A-M-S.'
They didn't know whether to laugh or cry.

Finally, one of the most delightful but shameful feelings of
all, one that we all have to keep under our hats: the feeling, when
bereaved, of being *special*. Being the centre of attention during
this wretched time can be positively addictive, and many people
spin out their grief not because they are unhappy but because
they cannot bear to lose this unique role. They want to milk it
for all they are worth. They enjoy the adrenalin high of grief,
and they enjoy being, perhaps for the only time in their lives, the
focus of all sympathetic attention, the receiver of letters, phone-
calls, new people trying to reach out to them. The mother of
Edie, who died of anorexia, warned against the seductive quali-
ties of this specialness.

> It is very precious but also, inevitably, temporary. You can't
> string it out and try to keep it going. If you try to cash in
> on it, thinking you're always going to be special because
> you've lost a kid, then I think you're in trouble and you're
> in danger of thinking that you for some reason have the
> monopoly on suffering; it is your credential. You are apt to
> be a bore, an embarrassment. People may avoid you. You
> may lose your friends.

But while it lasts – wow! Michael Tolkin, in *Among the Dead*,
described the feelings of his hero, Frank, who, when he burst
into tears after his wife's death, attracted the attention of his two
friends.

> Lowell massaged his shoulders, and Dockery patted him,
> awkwardly, yes, but also, Frank thought, for a little luck.
> Now Dockery could anticipate courage in a bad situation.
> He would always know that he could touch someone who
> had been electrified by tragedy, this force, this angel of
> death in whose wake everyone close was given a measure
> of charisma. At last, thought Frank, I am fascinating.

These almost indecent words, the idea that someone bereaved

by death should be touched for luck or even be given a measure of charisma, or be found 'fascinating', are surely ones that cannot fail to ring guilty bells with everyone who has been bereaved. Meeting death, being so close, is rather like an exaggerated version of having shaken hands with Elvis Presley: 'What was he like?' our friends might say. Our encounter with the bitter and mysterious majesty and cruelty of death also makes us extraordinary, for there is a romance about death – all death, even seedy, crummy death, not just heroic death – that few of us would like to admit to but that we all surely feel.

In writing about the death of a friend, Vernon Scannell described his feelings of grandeur at simply being the messenger of death.

> My sorrow was the swollen, prickly kind,
> Not handsome mourning, smartly cut and pressed:
> An actual grief, I swear. Therefore to find
> Myself engaged upon a shameful quest
> For anyone who'd known him, but who thought
> That he was still alive, was something strange.
> Something disquieting; for what I sought,
> Was power and presence beyond my usual range.
>
> For once my audience listened, welcomed me,
> Avid for every syllable that spoke
> Of woven fear and grieving. Nervously
> They eyed my black, ambassadorial cloak.
> Their faces greyed; my friend's death died, and they
> Saw theirs walk in alive. I felt quite well –
> Being Death's man – until they went away,
> And I was left with no one else to tell.

But the most socially unacceptable feeling that comes after death, perhaps, is not laughter, nor relief, nor blankness nor specialness – it is greed. It is not really greed; it is need. But it comes out like that, and society doesn't like it. When someone dies we look for something on to which we can pin our desperate longings. And, to compensate for the loss of our loved ones, we attach unusually great importance to objects and things. This obsession with things material is worthy of a chapter all of its own.

8. Wills and Things

Immediately after my father's death I was obsessed with the need to have things of his to remind me of him, to keep him alive in some way. I wanted to build a fortress of his books and clothes and pictures, and hide inside it ... I was anxious lest my stepmother failed to realize how important my father's belongings were to me, anxious lest other brothers and sisters took things I felt I needed. (Rebecca Abrams, *When Parents Die*)

After a death, the ideal bereaved people are assumed to have their heads well in the clouds of grief, longing, or some kind of spiritual sadness. Not for them the idle chatter of the cocktail party; not for them the material matters of this world; no, their tear-filled eyes are fixed on higher matters. It is loss and mortality that preoccupies them; for them the physical and material world should scarcely matter any more. They have had an encounter with death. They are grand and aloof, for some time at least, from the grimy, greedy, material world of us ordinary mortals.

As usual, so much nonsense. After a death, *things* are terribly important. Indeed, they may take on a whole new horrific significance – and yet, as usual, it is extremely difficult to convey this to the world at large, which marks you down, when you, say, tussle with your sister for your mother's flawed pearl necklace, as no more than a low-down greedy grabber who has completely forgotten, while you fight for a mere trinket, that your mother has died.

The truth is that after a death, things are no longer mere trinkets. Pieces of furniture are not bits of wood; money is not cash; houses are not bricks and mortar. The loved one has gone, so the possessions take on this mysterious meaning, as if they are the last link with the dead people, often becoming imbued with their very lost selves, talismans of their souls. There is a particular saucer, for instance, that 'is' my mother. Whenever I look at it, she's there. If someone else were to take it I would be furious, and fight for it. To outsiders it would seem as if I were squabbling over a cracked piece of china; I would actually be fighting for dear life for a part of *her*.

After he died, I asked my stepmother for a red spotted hand-kerchief belonging to my father. It was a symbol of everything he meant to me, a symbol of him. My stepmother gave me one, apologizing that it was a new one he had bought, and one he had never used. Naturally much of my father's magic was inevitably lost, since it was still crisp with cotton dressing, but after the feelings of disappointment I managed to invest it with some kind of paternal power, and kept it in my handbag. Two years later, in a fit of fury and unhappiness at what I felt was his treachery in abandoning me, I tore it up and threw it away. This scarlet spotted cotton square had taken the brunt of several strong emotions. It had been longed for, given disappointment, regained my love, and then had been destroyed. No one can tell me that it was 'just a handkerchief'.

In *Patrimony*, Philip Roth brilliantly describes how 'things' – in his case money – took on a completely different significance once it became clear that his father was going to die. In a fit of rationality and kindness, he had once told his father that he didn't need to be a beneficiary of his will and that any money should be left to Philip's brother, Sandy, who was, as a father with children, in greater need.

But now, with his death anything but remote, being told by him that he had gone ahead and, on the basis of my re-quest, substantially eliminated me as one of his heirs, eli-cited an unforeseen response: I felt repudiated – and the fact that his eliminating me from the will had been my own doing did not at all mitigate this feeling of having been cast out by him. I had made a generous gesture that was also, I suppose, of a piece with the assertions of equality and self-reliance that I had been making to my father since early adolescence. Admittedly, it was also a characteristic attempt to take the moral high ground within the family, to define myself in my fifties, as I had in college and graduate school and later as a young writer, as a son to whom material considerations were largely negligible – and I felt crushed from having done it: naïve and foolish and crushed.

To my great dismay, standing with him over his last will and testament, I discovered that I wanted my share of the financial surplus that, against all odds, had been accumulated over a lifetime by the obdurate, resolute father of mine. I wanted the money because it was his money and I was his son and I had a right to my share, and I wanted it because it was, if not an authentic chunk of his hard-working hide, something like the embodiment of all that he had overcome or outlasted. It was what he had to give me, it was what he had wanted to give me, it was due me by custom and tradition, and why couldn't I have kept my mouth shut and allowed what was only natural to prevail?

Didn't I think I deserved it? Did I consider my brother and his children more deserving inheritors than I, perhaps because my brother, by having given him grandchildren, was more legitimately a father's heir than was the son who had been childless? Was I a younger brother who suddenly had become unable to assert his claim against the seniority of someone who had been there first? Or, to the contrary, was I a younger brother who felt that he had encroached too much upon an older brother's prerogatives already? Just where had this impulse to cast off my right of inheritance come from, and how could it have so easily overwhelmed expectations that I now belatedly discovered a son was *entitled* to have?

Too proud to repudiate his own wishes, he was unable to tell his father his feelings.

It did not seem worth even the thirty or forty thousand dollars to establish the conditions for a family feud or the

eruption of poisonous feelings that is notoriously associated with the last-minute adjustment of an inheritance.

But his description shows how the things the dead person leaves
behind can have extraordinary and far-reaching significance,
significance that most people would barely credit.

I am certain that one of the reasons that wills are the subject
of so much hatred – as the old saying goes, when there's a will
there's a war – is because the possessions represent the love that
you have lost from the person who died. That is why beneficiaries can fight so hard over apparently trivial things. Why did
they get the books in his library when you only got the shelves?
Why did they get anything at all, indeed? Didn't he love you
best?

When someone dies, the first thought that often creeps unwelcome into a bereaved person's head is: 'How much will I get?'
Usually they put it, ashamed, out of their minds, ticking themselves off for being chilly, soulless creeps. But I think more
desperately emotional reasons prompt the thought. Faced with
someone who has died, you are left with a hole in your life. The
natural reaction is: 'How can I fill that hole?' The mind turns to
the will. How much they left you is a way of filling up the gap.
The money or property turns into a symbol of their love and
affection. People say: 'Don't get fussed over the will, it's only
money.' True as this may be in rational terms, the beneficiaries
often don't see it as 'only money'. They see their gifts as love,
love that will stop up the aching gap of loss.

One woman discovered that a necklace of her mother's that
she considered to be hers by right had been given to her
mother's cleaner.

It wasn't especially valuable, though the stones were real,
but I just couldn't let the thought of it go. One minute I'd
tell myself that the memory of my mother was enough,
and that I had lots of other pieces of her jewellery, and
what was a necklace anyway, and that this cleaner deserved
it as she had been so loyal to my mum over the years; the

next minute I'd be tormented with want, eaten up with resentment feeling that the necklace was *mine* and feeling that if I didn't have it I'd die. I'd ring up all my friends asking them how on earth I could get the necklace back without causing offence. I even rang my aunt who'd been responsible for giving this woman the necklace in the first place. She said she couldn't possibly ask for it back because the woman had been so incredibly grateful to get it. I would wake up at night, tormenting myself. Finally my son told me I just had to try to get it back, even if my request were refused. I went out and got a virtually identical necklace, rather more expensive actually, and sent it to this woman explaining the situation. She sent back the original necklace at once, with a lovely letter saying she completely understood. I can't tell you what it meant to me, getting that necklace back. I could sleep properly at last. I felt I had something of my mother's, and I knew my mother wanted me to have it.

Paula Yates, at the moment of writing, appears to be still in dispute with her father Jess's twenty-three-year-old girlfriend about the ownership of old copies of his *Saturday Evening Post*. Though a will can arouse tremendously strong emotions of bitterness, jealousy and resentment, it is always worth trying to remember, in the face of all that primitive rage, that the will was written at a certain time in someone's life, and didn't necessarily represent what they thought the moment they died, the week before they made the will, or even the week after. Carol Staudacher says about suicide notes:

It is important to put the note in perspective. That is, it is one item which reflects your loved one's thinking along a whole continuum of thought. The note is not necessarily representational of the same mind which conceived the suicide and carried it out. The note only represents your loved one's state of mind when the note was written. It is a mistake to try to extract the essence of the tragedy from this one piece of communication, however lucid it proves to be.

If you substitute the word 'will' for 'suicide note' it can help to shed a ray of rational sanity on to a situation that all too often is shot through with feelings of rage and disappointment. (Though what good a ray of rational sanity will be in a furnace of hunger and need, you may well ask.)

Some possessions retain their magical symbolism for years – pets, for instance, may 'hold' the existence of a loved one until they die. Others may simply act as transitional objects, helping people slowly to integrate the fact of a bereavement into their lives.

Transitional objects are usually seen as cuddlies for children, which comfort them when their mothers leave for short periods, symbolizing the security they miss. But they exist for bereaved people, too. One psychologist believes these types of linking objects are used to handle separation anxiety and that they provide a 'token of triumph' over the loss. He believes that linking objects mark a blurring of psychic boundaries between the bereaved person and the one mourned, as if representations of the two persons or parts of them merge externally through their use.

Objects can bring great comfort, even in bed when bereaved partners can feel particularly lonely. Many is the widower who has popped a couple of pillows into his wife's nightdress and cuddled it to sleep. Many is the widow who has hugged a teddy-bear or hot-water bottle in longing, sleeping with her head on her husband's pyjamas.

It's not uncommon, too, for people to attend funerals in the dead person's clothes. They go to the funeral to mourn; they wear the dead person's clothes for comfort. It is a bizarre paradox to say goodbye to someone while hanging on to them, but most people will understand Blake Morrison's feelings when he described his father's funeral. Going through his father's wardrobe before the ceremony, he feels like a grave-robber. I take three jumpers, a dozen pairs of socks, two pairs of brown leather shoes, some cuff-links, and stash them in an old RAF travel-bag of his. Then I put on his white nylon shirt, black tie, grey suit, black woollen socks, black shoes. I am going to the funeral in his clothes.

Before the service he was advised that his father's pacemaker would explode in the crematorium while being burnt. Blake Morrison asked for it, and during the funeral he held the retrieved pacemaker in his pocket.

I clutch the pleasant plasticity of its side, as if it were a precious stone – the talisman of my old man. I put it in my trouser pocket to fondle through the funeral, not letting go.

Though I didn't wear my mother's clothes to her memorial service, I had an extremely odd experience. A fashion guru, my mother had only worn black, white and scarlet. Looking in the mirror before I left, I saw myself, scarlet-lipsticked, in a black hat, white shirt, and yellow skirt. Something seemed terribly wrong, until I changed the skirt for black. It was only when I went up the aisle to read the lesson and heard the gasps from the congregation that I realized that I had got myself up to look exactly like my mother. And as I realized it, I felt I even became her. I felt I was doing something shocking – perhaps I had dressed like her to comfort myself, but in my case I think I had dressed like her to literally step into her shoes. I could almost hear a victorious little voice inside me screaming: 'You're dead and I'm alive, and I'm you now, and everyone's looking at me, not you any more!' And why not?

As objects can change what they mean once a person has died, and take on greater significance – so, also, can they lose significance. Two years after her husband died, a widow was happy to put her house on the market. 'Now Bill's not here, and the children have grown up, all the fun has gone out of it. It's just a building now.' And a designer who begged to photograph the flat of a woman of exceptional taste and chic, after she died, was disappointed when he went round with his camera.

Even though she had only died two days before, it was curious how tatty and dusty the flat looked. Even though she had been bedridden for a year, she still seemed to imbue everything in it with her fascinating presence, even the rooms that she hadn't been in for months. Of course the flat was still beautiful when I photographed it, but it lacked the eccentric excitement it had when she was alive.

When Hugo Williams divided the spoils after a relative had died, he found that the meaning in the objects left behind constantly shifted. Describing this in the *Daily Mail*, he wrote:

One of the few mitigating factors of a loved one's death is that you get their things. They are best shared out soon so the bereaved can get the benefit of this minimal compensation. We either gave things to each other which we thought we would like, or modestly held things up and said: 'Does anyone want this?' – then sadly added them to our own pile. If more than one person wanted something we tossed for it, hoping secretly that we wouldn't get it, since it would always be reaching out to someone else.

The share-out, accompanied by champagne, was fun while it lasted – like a sort of nightmare Christmas – if not afterwards, when we found ourselves alone with our newly acquired goods. Why did everything have about it an air of ill-gotten gains? All the bereaved's LPs, for instance, original cast recordings of *Kiss Me Kate*, *Guys and Dolls*, *Carousel*, *Wonderful Town*, *The Pyjama Game*, *West Side Story*, pre-rock Broadway musicals which we grew up with, are all unplayable for the foreseeable future as far as I am concerned, unless I become even unhappier than they are ... Their presence will prove we are life members of the senior generation, the next in line for the chop. It won't be long before they are something which used to belong to us.

Whether we like it or not, they will go on muttering their old owners' names for as long as we have them, insisting on a certain respect. Ownership will go on being deferred backwards until we pass them on ourselves, at which point they will finally become 'ours' – in the eyes of our children at least. Now that a certain longed-for cigar-cutter has become 'mine' it exudes a curiously negative appeal. I agreed with my brother when he said he didn't mind who kept the pictures as long as he could look at them from time to time; that way they had a chance of hanging on to a little of their old charisma. All the same, it's hard to stop yourself grabbing something when it seems to be, literally, the chance of a lifetime.

There is, as always, the opposite reaction, too. Some people feel extremely ambivalent about receiving anything from a will. They feel that getting something from a death implies they have collaborated with death. Such is the strange way our minds work.

But 'things' are not just left to us in wills. When someone dies, they will, however tidy they have been, have left things around. These can shock or comfort. Depending on how you feel, what mood you are in and the myriad other factors that make our bereaved responses change from day to day, bumping into objects that remind us of the dead person may bring either comfort that the dead person is present, or misery because the encounter reminds us they have gone for ever. Mostly they bring both feelings – 'Now you've got him, now you haven't got him' – and when one follows the other, the bereaved feel extremely depressed and sad. And confused.

After I had visited the hospital to collect my mother's bits and pieces after she died, I wrote in my diary:

They weren't just my mother's effects in the plastic bag the hospital gave me. There was something almost tangible which was not my mother as well. The glimpse of her scarlet dressing-gown cord slipping out of the top of the bag was a reminder. It was like looking at life as a black and white negative; Mummy seemed like one of those white shapes, all shadows in reverse. Print it up and there is a sparkling, smiling figure against a pale background; but in negative the background is black and the person is only defined by shadows of absence. But still there. Not gone.

Keith Collins, Derek Jarman's friend, was quoted by Pauline Peters in the *Evening Standard* as saying, after Derek died of AIDS:

> It's not the obvious things that upset me. One cold day I thought I'd test myself and put on Derek's coat. I felt nothing. Then I put my hand in the pocket and I found a 20p he'd left there and for some reason that set me off. I was crying my eyes out for hours.

With advanced technology the dead may leave even closer reminders of themselves, as well. Not just fading black and white photos, but glimpses of themselves on video; most poignantly they leave their own recorded message on the answering machine. It is a bold close relative who scrubs that out or, more peculiarly, though understandably, leaves it on.

The task that most bereaved people dread getting down to is sorting through the dead person's 'effects' as they are called. This is a moment when 'things' scream out their differing messages, deafening the bereaved person with shouts of what they represent. How difficult it is to throw away their old toothbrush. How impossible to chuck that ghastly coat of his that he loved – that you had been trying to give to a jumble sale for years; the stupid, filthy frying pan of which she was so fond; his pipe; her make-up. Then there are even more personal reminders – hair on their clothes, dandruff on the jacket-shoulder, even the grimy mark of an unwashed collar or a slightly greasy patch left by their hair on the bedhead, the half-moon of a nail-clipping discovered under the bed – and always the deeply personal smell of all their clothes.

Dealing with the dead person's effects is handled in three ways – chucking, keeping and slow-chucking. Slow-chuckers complete the task eventually, but it can often take years. A widow may take a fortnight to clear just one drawer of her husband's desk, every object examined and fondled before the big decision is made of whether to keep it or chuck it – or, sometimes most difficult, give it away (to someone who might not appreciate it?).

The keepers are like Queen Victoria who, when her husband Albert died, kept everything of his intact, demanding that his clothes and his shaving gear be laid out exactly as he wished them morning and night. She went round the Palace actually talking to him as if he were alive. This is known as 'mummification' and is most often done by parents of children who have died. Sometimes they keep their children's bedrooms intact for years. It's thought that in the back of their mind they don't really accept that the person is actually dead, and they are waiting for them to return.

Wendy Parry, mother of Tim Parry, killed by an IRA bomb, was quoted in *The Times* shortly after his death. Every morning she glanced at Tim's school portrait which she and her husband, Colin, had hung in the hall. 'As I pass it I say "Good morning, Tim." And every night before I go up to bed I wish him "Good night" . . .' Colin has long and tearful conversations with Tim's portrait when everyone else is in bed. Wendy and Colin regularly watch a video of him, an audio specialist having lifted the sound of his voice from the soundtrack so that they can listen to the tape in the car. They plan to turn a room into a place filled with Tim's memorabilia, because, Colin says: 'I want a room full of warm and happy memories of our son. I will never let go of the tangible things. I find myself clutching his clothes to my face and I can still smell him. I feel his presence there very strongly.'

In *Father's Place*, a widow described how her child would 'wrap herself in her father's travelling rug for no other reason than that it had belonged to him. She would smooth her hand over his tobacco box as though it gave off some kind of curative balm. She would lay her cheek against his coat hanging in the hall.' The smaller children made an imaginary companion out of him. 'They made room for him on the sofa, saved cake for him and included him in all their games.' A friend said she was getting like Queen Victoria, supposing she laid her late husband's dressing-gown out on his bed every night as she did for years after Prince Albert died. 'I told her I didn't because I wore it myself. My own had split at the seams and his was nearly new. The girls were wearing his white sweaters for games at school.' A girl who spoke to Jill Krementz said: 'When my father died we put his clothes in some boxes and put them up in the attic. I keep some of his colognes on my dresser for decoration. They remind me of him – the way he used to smell.'

We each have our own ways of coping and if keeping objects helps, then keep; if chucking helps, then chuck. Psychologists would have us believe that those who keep everything are trying to deny that anything has happened; and guess what they say about people who chuck everything out? Yup. They, too, are denying. They are either rewriting history ('He was a useless partner, really, so let's get rid of him because I don't really miss him') or denying the existence of the person in the first place. One man refuses to have his wife's name mentioned in the house, or have any pictures of her in the home at all, despite the fact that he still cares for their two young children. He has even asked that his in-laws remove the photographs they have when he goes round to see them. And Philip Roth describes how his father went on a wild chucking spree after his wife's death. After burying his mother, Roth came back home with family and friends to find that his father had arrived first and had already disappeared into his mother's bedroom where he started furiously throwing things out.

Not even my opening the bedroom door and coming into the room and firmly saying, 'Dad, what are you doing?' did anything to slow him down. The bed was already strewn with dresses, coats, skirts and blouses pulled from the closet, and he was now busily chucking things from a corner of her lowest bottom drawer into a plastic garbage bag. I put my hand on his shoulder and gripped it forcefully. 'People are here for you,' I said; 'they want to see you, to talk to you —' 'What good is this stuff anymore? It's no good to me having it there. This stuff can go to Jewish relief — it's in mint condition —' 'Stop, please — just stop. There's time for all this later. We'll do it together later. Stop throwing things out,' I said. 'Pull yourself together. Go into the living-room where you're needed.'

But he *was* pulled together. He didn't appear to be either in a daze or in the throes of a hysterical fit — he was simply doing what he had done all his life: the next difficult job. Thirty minutes before, we had buried her body; now to dispose of her things . . .

It was my father's primitivism that stunned me. Standing all alone emptying her drawers and her closets, he seemed driven by some instinct that might be natural to a wild beast or an aboriginal tribesman but ran counter to just about every mourning rite that had evolved in civilized societies to mitigate the sense of loss among those who survive the death of a loved one. Yet there was also something almost admirable in this pitilessly realistic determination to acknowledge, instantaneously, that he was now an old man living alone and that symbolic relics were no substitute for the real companion of fifty-five years. It seemed to me that it was not out of fear of her things and their ghost-like power that he wanted to rid the apartment of them without delay — to bury *them* now, too — but because he refused to sidestep the most brutal of all facts.

9. They Don't Know What to Say

The loss of a loved one ... can only partially be shared ... the work of mourning is by its very nature something which takes place in the watches of the night and in the solitary recesses of the mind. (Anthony Storr)

Bereavement is an internal feeling. But happy internal feelings – perhaps finding a warm ray of spiritual comfort in a winter landscape, or feeling surprisingly touched by the kind gesture of a stranger – are usually kept private, cherished and hugged secretly, like treasure. Because the feeling of bereavement is so painful we naturally look to others to help us in our confusion. But because bereavement is such a personal and internal state, and because we feel super-vulnerable and sensitive, it is extremely difficult for anyone outside us to be able to help us in any way at all.

We look for succour from people who are, through no fault of their own, unable to give it. There is hardly any help to give, anyway, except perhaps a hug, a listening ear, practical help, and the very chance remark that may trigger something within ourselves that temporarily eases some of the muddle and pain. To the vulnerable bereaved, most people can appear to be clodhopperingly insensitive. Like children trying to help you cook a meal, their attempts to help may be touching, but in the end they may only make the whole thing worse.

There are the extreme reactions from people who are simply so terrified of the feelings that bereavement brings up in themselves that they would just prefer you go away. C. S. Lewis wrote: 'I'm aware of being an embarrassment to everyone I meet ... perhaps the bereaved ought to be isolated in special settlements, like lepers.'

This public horror of death reveals itself in the announcements in the Deaths column in *The Times*. The word 'died' is only rarely used. Ninety-five per cent of the announcements run along the lines of: 'Brown – Tom, beloved father of Susan, suddenly at home on Wednesday . . .' or 'Jones – on October 11th peacefully in hospital, George, much-loved husband of Pam . . .' These sentences are meaningless. Tom Brown could just as easily have been finishing the crossword at home on Wednesday, and George Jones could just as easily have recovered in hospital as died there. One day perhaps we will regard this style of announcing a death as bizarre as the Victorian habit of coyly referring to chicken-legs as drumsticks.

'When my husband died I went round to my sister,' said one widow. 'She had, I know, been devastated by the death of our mother two years before, but I wasn't expecting her reaction as I walked through the door. "Don't bring your grief here!" she said. I walked out and have not spoken to her since.' Perhaps this woman could not cope with her own feeling of bereavement being roused, like a sleeping dragon, from its cave; perhaps she, like many other people, simply found it incredibly difficult to deal with other people's emotions. It isn't because they're unkind. They're just shy, embarrassed or tormented by the experience of another person's tears or rage. They think that if they mention the death you will get upset and, as they don't wish to upset you, they keep quiet. But what they don't realize is that the bereaved person is just dying to talk.

'Some people think if you don't talk about it you won't think about it,' said one bereaved parent. 'In fact if you do talk about it you will be quicker able to stop thinking about it constantly. We would go out with people and they wouldn't even bring up the topic. But it was all we wanted to talk about and nothing else.' Jenny Danks is a television producer and actress, and was quoted in the *Independent on Sunday*, in an interview by Catherine Millner. When she was at school, her mother committed suicide; she returned home and her father told her the news.

I tried to scream, and I know this sounds awful but they

tried to put their hands over my mouth. There must have been a doctor there because I can remember they gave me some tranquillizers, which I think is completely the wrong thing to do, but it wasn't their fault, it was just ignorance . . . The one thing I remember is my aunt saying the next day, 'Would you like to go and have your hair cut?' I looked at her and just thought, 'You're mad! Here I am, my world has just fallen apart – how can I possibly go and sit in the hair-dresser's? How could that possibly make any difference?'

Fear may make some people shy away from a bereaved person: fear of emotion but also fear of anger and rage – which is often dished out to anyone within shouting, spitting or hitting distance – or, worse, fear of longing. The utter craven helpless-ness of a bereaved person, the sobbing and the clinging, the cries of: 'But how can I live without him? I'm so lonely! Help me!' may scare off the bereaved's friends, who, terrified of becom-ing too involved, back off. After her father had died, Rebecca Abrams wrote:

Mum's dependency leaves me cold. She is like a child, un-aware, incapable of nearly everything and always needing care and support and encouragement. The sight of her so weak and vulnerable frightens me, makes me back off emo-tionally. She often says how glad she is that we are close, that I am the only one who can understand how she feels, but I don't feel close at all. I hate her dependency. I find it revolting. I can't talk to her. I don't want her emotion. But I feel guilty because I should be helping her if I can. I can't talk to her anymore. There is no one in the world for me to talk to now. I can't go to her and tell her how desperate I feel. She is the most dear person in the world to me and I try not to shut her up, but her needing me frightens me so much.

It's thought that one reason that widows have been known to have been shunned by married female friends is because other women fear the strength of what they imagine to be their strong sexual longings. Obviously, for some people, sexual feelings simply shut down tightly after a bereavement; but others may be tormented with desire. They dread their worst fear – that they may never have sex with anyone again. Many is the widow or widower who has succumbed to a comforting one-night stand even before the funeral, only to be tormented with guilt later.

Sometimes people around a bereaved person keep away simply because they hate the sight of blood, as it were. Bereaved people are often desperate to go into every gory aspect of a death, and will happily describe the event in minute detail – detail which can turn the stomach of their listeners. This writer describes a miscarriage. I think she describes it well and movingly, but others have said that it makes them feel sick.

> After a miscarriage at home – a small jelly-like sac appearance. It was my baby and I just held it in my hand. It looked so perfect in its little sac of fluid. I can't describe the feelings I had, sat in the bathroom looking at it, the sadness and despair were overwhelming. I went back to bed. I'd put the baby in an empty face cream jar and hid it in my handbag and then went to tell my husband. We cried for hours, we just held each other in bed and shared our grief.

They went to the hospital, where they were told it was just a mucus plug and to go home and stop being silly.

> I tried to point out to her that you could clearly see the baby but she wasn't interested. We drove back to my in-laws' house in silence, both too stunned to speak. When we got home I asked my husband to look at it. I was sure I was right and that it was the baby. So we tipped it out of the jar and on the work-top in the kitchen the little sac burst and there lay our tiny baby. I stood and looked at it for a long time and then without thinking we cleaned it up into the kitchen paper and put it in the bin. I wish we'd treated it

with a little more respect and maybe even secretly buried it in the garden. It seemed such an undignified end to such a precious life. I'm empty and heartbroken. I keep wanting to talk about it but no one will listen. They say it's too morbid.

If you, too, squirm at that story, don't criticize anyone, if you're bereaved, who crosses to the other side of the street. They may think you're going to tell them all the gory details of your loved one's final hours.

Some people find it hard to listen or talk about a bereavement because it brings up such painful personal memories. A report in the *Independent on Sunday* told how, when one woman's father was dying, and she mentioned this to her boss, her boss would say: 'How terrible, I can't bear it. Don't talk about it.' After her father died a few days later on Christmas Eve, she went back to work in the New Year.

I found a note on my desk saying 'Why are you so many hours down this month? Please come and see Admin immediately.' No one had been told my father had died. People were coming up to me and saying: 'Where have you been? Did you have a nice holiday?' My boss couldn't face me. She didn't come to see me until about five o'clock in the afternoon. She didn't know what to say, she told me. I didn't want her to say anything in particular, I just wanted her to put her head round the door and say 'Hi.'

It turned out that this behaviour wasn't malicious. Her boss's father had died some years earlier and she had never come to terms with it. She was so paralysed by the situation that she couldn't even bring herself to let her employee's colleagues know what was happening, which led to the upsetting note and comments on her return.

The cruel silence that can follow a bereavement can be just as hurtful as the crassest of remarks. It can feel more like a physical assault than absence of sympathy. There are days when – even fifteen months and the safe arrival of a new baby later – the pain and grief feel just as bad as the day the miscarriage happened, and I wonder, if time is the great healer, how much is needed,' said one mother whose child was stillborn.

One thing that has upset me since our new baby was born and which hurts is the number of people who have sent cards and congratulated us and yet never said 'sorry' about Matthew, even though they knew. I realize they were probably embarrassed and didn't know what to say, but just a quick 'sorry to hear' would have been nice. People also refer to Alex as our first, which hurts. I really wish they would acknowledge Matthew and not pretend he never existed.

Maria Cantacuzino tells of the reaction after her brother died.

There were friends who shrank back unable to handle my grief which they saw as distressing and demanding. Many, who were supportive at the time, later stopped allowing me to talk about it. I could see the shutters come down at the merest hint of the subject. I know my mother felt this even more keenly than me, and when over ten years later I had to interview several bereaved mothers and fathers for an article on the subject, every one of them mentioned the fact that people wouldn't allow them to talk about it. Shortly after my brother's death I discovered a poem written by my mother hidden away in a drawer. It contained these lines:

'The storm in the dream and the tears on my cheek
are tidied away during the day
folded like my nightdress under the pillow.'

And yet, despite the deeply personal nature of the feelings, despite the near-impossibility of anyone being able to 'get right' a response, we try, like moths around a flame, to confide, to open up to people, to explain, to repeat, to share, to find some kind of balm from someone outside, even if it's just an acknow-ledgement that we have been bereaved. C. S. Lewis wrote: 'I like best the well brought-up young men, almost boys, who walk up to me as if I were a dentist, turn very red, get it over, and then edge away to the bar as quickly as they decently can.' He's right. These are the best. Because when we do communicate our feel-ings after bereavement, if we don't get silence or fear, we almost certainly get the wrong response. Eighty-five per cent of the time you receive what you feel is a verbal slap in the face – all the worse because it's not intended as such; it's intended as kindness. The truth is that *very few people are good sympathizers when it comes to death.* Thus, the well-meaning but incredibly hurtful remarks of other people are yet another burden the bereaved have to bear. Since the bereaved are super-sensitive, if anyone gives them a piece of advice that is just the tiniest bit off-key, they are extra-quick to take offence.

The following collection of 'helpful' remarks was gathered with the help of two widows who consoled themselves in their bereavements by compiling, between them, a notebook contain-ing the most kindly but insensitive remarks made by well-wishers.

'You'll get over it.' Just a remark like that may be offered as comfort – and received with rage. How dare anyone suggest I will *ever* get over it! How dare they tell me how I will feel!

'Remember, he died peacefully. It's something to be thankful for.' How dare you concentrate on *his* experience when you should be concentrating on *mine!* I don't care how peacefully he died, it's the fact he died at all that upsets me! It is obscene to suggest there is anything to be 'thankful for' in his death!

'You have suffered so much you should go away and have a good rest. You need a holiday.' How dare you suggest a holiday could help this grief at all! I would simply be unhappy and alone in a foreign country! You just want to get rid of me!

'Death doesn't matter . . . there is no death . . .' It does matter. And you might as well say there is no birth, or birth doesn't matter.

'Time will heal.' I don't want time to heal. Time was what got me into this fine mess to start with. Stop the clocks or, better still, put them back. Anyway, time doesn't heal, you big fool. It is what happens to you during the passage of time that is the point, not the time itself.

'I know how you feel . . .' You have *no idea* how I feel!

'You're doing marvellously . . . You're so strong.' Don't be patronizing, anyway, you have no idea how I'm 'doing' as you call it.

'Keep your chin up. He wouldn't like you to be unhappy.' Well, he is not around, is he, or perhaps you hadn't noticed? So there is very little point in behaving as if he were.

'This has brought you all closer together.' *I'll* be the judge of that, thank you!

'She was such a terrific person, I knew her for such a long time and she was marvellous . . .' Your experiences of her make no difference to me. Can't you think of anyone except yourself? What about me?

'At least he died happy . . .' This is the sort of remark that was made to Lady MacMillan, after the death of her husband, choreographer Kenneth MacMillan, during a performance. She said:

> One of the things that made me angry was a woman at a dinner party some time later, saying to me wasn't it marvellous that he died with his boots on? She went on about history being made, about it being absolutely wonderful. I said bugger that, I'd rather have him *in* his boots in the kitchen drinking his endless cups of tea and I suspect he would prefer that as well. I have lost my temper on a couple of occasions in the most appalling way. I've had a very short fuse this year.

'You must put it to one side now and look to the future . . .' You must keep your mouth shut and stop telling other people to do impossible things. How would you feel if I told you that you 'must win the women's bobsleighing race in the Winter

Olympics'? You would look at me as if I were suggesting a crazy impossibility, as I am looking at you now.

'You're only young . . .' So? I've got brown hair. I'm only five foot six. What the fuck difference does being young make?

'He had a good life . . .' So what? If anything it makes it worse. If he had had a bad life we could all rejoice at his passing.

'It's all for the best . . .' Maybe, but that is not for you to say.

'You are lucky to have such a large, close family . . .' Lucky? Did I hear you right? Did you use the word 'lucky' in connection with me, the unluckiest person in the whole, wide world?

'It was "meant" . . .' It was also 'meant' that I should punch you on the nose if you made a ridiculous remark like that.

'When my mother died, I felt . . .' Could you tell me another time, please? It's *my* bereavement we're talking about now, not yours.

'At least you have your writing/children/painting/work . . .' But I had them all before *and* I had the dead person alive. It's like saying to someone whose hands have been chopped off, 'At least you have your feet.'

The most insensitive remark that was made to me after my father's death was by a 'friend' of his who kindly explained that the reason he had died was because he took too little exercise and ate too much salt. My breath was taken away.

Confusingly, however, what is one person's crass remark is another's words of wisdom. 'My mother was incredibly comforted when a friend of hers told me that though my father was dead, their marriage wasn't over,' said one son. 'Now to me that was utter rubbish. If she had told me that though my father was dead I still had a father, or that I was still his son, I would have had great difficulty in controlling my temper. But my mother found real solace from this weird piece of "wisdom".'

There is another group of people who may not make remarks that unwittingly give offence, but who can do other kinds of harm. These are the ones who are over-anxious to comfort. At the first drop of blood, they whip out antiseptic, gauze, sticking plaster, crêpe bandages, plaster cast, splint and a pair of crutches. These are the ones who are so desperate to divert you from your misery that after a chat with them you come away feeling frustrated, bottled up and, since you find it hard to feel angry with them because they have apparently been so kind, angry with yourself for not being able to accept their 'kindness'.

Giving way to grief is stigmatized as weak, indulgent, pessimistic, and friends often feel their role is to try to jolly the mourner out of this gloomy frame of mind as soon as possible. And a counsellor commented that:

> Confronted with someone needing to cry out their grief or shake off their fear, we are likely to intervene to interrupt the emotional release and calm the distressed person down, thus becoming more comfortable ourselves, while leaving them with their feelings of distress intact.

Other people find it so difficult to stand simply witnessing our pain that, rather than let it flare up and die down naturally, they would prefer to cover the flames with damp blankets of comfort. The action leaves a horrible, stifling, singed smell. They are doing us no favours at all. They are, rather, distracting us from something important. Painful, perhaps, but true, and interesting. As Iris Murdoch wrote:

> Outsiders often help bereaved people by reminding them that they have urgent duties and must not remain in still contemplation of what is uniquely terrible. There are immediate tasks, arrangements to be made, others to be comforted, ordinary life at last to be carried on. Can less extreme lessons enable us to take in our mortality and see the world in its light? Can it be done through art, through meditation, through psychoanalysis, through reading books or listening to preaching?

No, she concludes. And others shouldn't try to stick clumsy plasters on to wounds that will only heal in their own good time. Then there are those ghastly people who try to reason you

out of feeling dreadful. Pull yourself together. You're not the
only one to have suffered a bereavement. Death comes to us all.
After Hamlet's father has died, his mother urges him to:

> Cast thy nighted colour off . . .
> Do not for ever with thy vailed lids
> Seek for thy noble father in the dust.
> Thou know'st 'tis common – all that lives must die,
> Passing through nature to eternity.

His uncle joins in, with more manipulative pressure:

> 'Tis sweet and commendable in your nature, Hamlet,
> To give these mourning duties to your father;
> But you must know your father lost a father;
> That father lost lost his and the survivor bound,
> In filial obligation, for some term
> To do obsequious sorrow. But to persever
> In obstinate condolement is a course
> Of impious stubbornness; 'tis unmanly grief;
> It shows a will most incorrect to heaven,
> A heart unfortified, a mind impatient,
> . . . Fie! 'tis a fault to heaven,
> A fault against the dead, a fault to nature,
> To reason most absurd; whose common theme
> Is death of fathers.

Charming.

Obviously there are some people who do manage to offer
comfort and help successfully, but most people only remember
the times when such sympathy was either misguided or patronizing. In *Father's Place*, the author wrote:

Another well-wisher told me it was time I stopped being
married to a ghost. I tried to explain that being married to
the ghost of someone you admired was not such a terrible
thing, particularly for his children. I believe that drawing
attention to the things that I admire in him: honesty, sym-

pathy, consideration for other people, a sense of humour, high spirits, a gentle voice, and so on – will help them in life much more than if I never mentioned him.

Finally there is a group of people who peddle a different line altogether. Far from trying to make you stop grieving, by comforting or distracting you, they almost feed on your grief. These are the bereavement vultures, the emotional coffin-riders, who not only get off on being associated with someone special – you, as a bereaved person – but who also revel in their role of sympathizers. They will not get off the phone, they ask you round and fix psychic vacuum cleaners on to your heart and eyes, trying to force tears out of you so that they can get off on comforting you. They are usually quick to ram their own ideas of what they like to think of as the 'grieving process' down your throat. When Susan Hill's baby died, she wrote:

> The counsellor herself even telephoned me later that day and urged me to make an appointment to see her to discuss my grief, to expose ways of dealing properly with my pain – all that sort of jargon. 'I'm sure you will find it beneficial, there are so many ways we have of helping you through the process of bereavement nowadays. Let us expose your grief together.' Her voice oozed sympathy and professional concern. I recoiled. I felt that she was invading my privacy, intruding tactlessly by assuring me I would feel all the better for her ministrations. Yes, of course I was over-reacting and being oversensitive. The bereaved always are. I have been appalled at the hungry way in which professional bereavement counsellors with all the psychological and sociological answers have peddled their wares so publicly in the aftermath of recent mass tragedies.

The Reverend 'Seye Olumide, whose five children died in a fire, also criticized those people who dictated ways of feelings to the bereaved. In an article, 'The Unexpected Death of Children through Disaster – a Personal View', he wrote:

There is a group of people, professionals and lay, who are 'fussers'. They wish to inform the bereaved of the expected emotional and dietary needs. Crying is good. Eating is excellent. Tea is particularly beneficial. You must talk about it. Alcohol is essential but only in moderation. Not crying is a symptom of repressed emotion or delayed shock, and most unhealthy. Thought is distorted in the newly bereaved, so let's assume they are invalids, and self-determination is very much frowned upon. They are going to go mad.

I dispute all this. Crying is wonderful for the human body (if you are able to, I could not) either alone or in the arms of loving and caring friends and relatives. It is not essential to 'perform' in public. Food is often unessential for days and the stomach is a good regulator of need. Tea, coffee, water, fruit juice are good but have no curative powers. Alcohol is an allowable weakness when over-indulged in on infrequent occasions. Not crying may mean many things ranging from being too busy (with immediate practical problems) to not wishing to cry in the presence of total strangers . . .

But if strangers, even professional strangers, are so unhelpful, what about the immediate family? They know a bereaved person better than anyone. They can surely help.

Yes . . . but.

I have often had letters like this one: 'I still feel so upset after my mother died two years ago. My husband was marvellous, but he doesn't quite understand, he doesn't like to see me upset, even he is getting fed up with me, I cry alone and dry my tears before he comes back from work.'

Sometimes the closer the relatives the less able are they to give comfort, for they too are grieving – for someone else. As Rachel Nickell's partner said to Lynda Lee-Potter in the *Daily Mail*, after Rachel was murdered:

It's very difficult for us because we're grieving for different people. Her parents are grieving for their child who played with the rabbit. I'm grieving for the woman I was going to share the rest of my life with, and they're not always the same person. At this level of pain, when somebody else doesn't understand what you feel, it adds to the hurt. Families can get really torn apart because everybody's got different needs.

One woman whose husband was an alcoholic and schizophrenic felt like kicking his gravestone while her children wept for him. It made her feel terribly guilty.

And the bereaved person can look for things in their close relatives and partners which they cannot ever fulfil. When their mother dies, they may look to their wives to fulfil a maternal role. When a husband dies a widow may look to a son to fulfil the role of a spouse in comforting her. When they don't come up with the goods, as they cannot, the bereaved person feels cut off, and misunderstood. Georgina Monckton's daughter died of a brain tumour three days before her second birthday, and she wrote about the experience.

> The death of a child puts enormous strain on a marriage. Piers [her husband] loved Isobel – she was his life – but he didn't want to bring her up in conversation, while all I wanted to do was talk about her. He would say: 'She's dead. She isn't here any more. You've got to concentrate on Emily [their other child].' There were times when I could have packed my suitcase and walked away . . . Rows started with Piers because we were coping in totally different ways. At one point when I was terribly distraught, instead of giving me a hug, he shook me, telling me once more that Isobel was dead and I was never going to see her again . . .

Writing about his feelings after his wife, Margie, had died, Goronwy Rees wrote:

> My family think me callous because I will not speak about her but if they would only understand the saddest thing

about dying is that the dead, having gone out of existence, can have no life at all, no feelings, no rights or duties, no claims. If it were not for that it would not be sad at all. But my family do not see this and so, while missing the real tragedy, wear themselves out all the more because they grieve for her as if she were alive and that is like throwing oneself against a brick wall, because the dead can't respond at all . . . I cried this week. Crying is the most terrible and shameful thing there is, at least to me, because I feel humiliated, and I will never cry again, whatever happens. But nothing worse than what has happened can ever happen again.

Certainly I found it very difficult, when my father died, to explain to people close to me how lonely I felt. Quite naturally they felt: 'How could she feel lonely, when she's got me?' But one does feel lonely, and particularly lonely when there is no one to tell how lonely you are, or when the people you'd like to tell might take offence.

(It has to be said, however, that for those living with bereaved people it is extremely difficult to get things right. The bereaved are touchy, liable to explode with tears or anger at any moment, and their reactions can continue, in an apparently arbitrary way, for years after the event. Frances Partridge admitted that she was relieved to reach a time when 'I'm not rejecting everything, as a telephone-box rejects foreign or worn coins.')

Children, as long as they are not too unhappy themselves, can often be the best sympathizers and healers. The father of little Alex, the son of Rachel Nickell, described how he behaved. 'He was doing some extraordinary things during those first few days. He made me sit at the top of the stairs and he got the Hoover out. He put the brush on my chest and said: "You've got a pip in your heart and I'm going to take it out."'

But in some families you can even find competitors for grief in the same way that they competed for love when the person was alive. 'I'm more unhappy than you!' 'No, I'm more unhappy than you!' 'I'm going to buy the biggest wreath because I'm really miserable!' 'No, we'll be civilized and all join together to buy one big wreath . . .' (But secretly I'm going to pop in a little bunch of violets just from me, because I'm mourning most.)

Then there are the emotional squabbles. If a young wife dies, with no children, who arranges the funeral? Her husband? Or her mother? When it comes to grieving, who is the Main Man? Who walks first down the aisle? Is it fair that it's usually only the Top Griever who gets the condolence letters? Thus the wife might get a huge pile, but the children, and his brothers and sisters, might get only a trickle.

With the condolence letters we can start to look at the more positive side, and the ways in which bereaved people *do* find the most help and comfort from other people. It is not so much what the people say in these letters – though they rarely dare put into writing the kind of fatuous remarks they say – but the fact that they have pulled out a sheet of paper, got out their pens, written something down, stuffed it into an envelope, stuck a stamp on it and put it in the postbox. It is this *act of letter-writing* that is the comfort, far more than the content. 'The comfort lies in the fact that the pile of letters indicated your grief has some importance, however brief,' wrote Mary Stott. Letters are tangible evidence of the life you led together.

After my father's death I will never let another death go by without dropping the relatives a line. Letters that say things like: 'He will live on forever in your heart' – trite lines I'd usually wrinkle a lip at – seemed to have huge significance, laden with meaning. 'I am down the road if you want an ear,' came from an old schoolfriend I barely knew. Certainly, despite my aches and pains, my step always got lighter at the top of the last flight of stairs when I saw that there was a pile of condolence letters waiting to be read. One friend wrote: 'These sad losses are signposts to new and different routes.' Another, comforting in its very ambiguousness: 'We share the mystery of his passing.' And:

'He'll be with you in your mind and memory of small things – a sort of pragmatic form of immortality, perhaps.'

Certain friends can help, too, simply by being there. And if they, too, have been bereaved, they do appear to be physical proof that a bereavement can be borne. They might even be able to help a bit with advice. 'I remember that particular corridor!' they can tell you. 'Beware – it gets very narrow at the end.' Or, 'Hey, I'm over here, watch out for that swamp you're getting to!' Or, 'There's an extra step there, don't slip – you may think you're on dry land, but you're not, it's quicker than you think over that bit, don't take that wrong turning . . .'

Good friends are people who don't mind hearing the details of the death again and again and again. Good friends are people who give you a hug and say, 'I'm so sorry. I don't know what to say,' instead of dreaming up a platitude. Good friends would never say you were lucky to have a large, warm family, they'd say they were glad you had a large, warm family – quite a different matter. Good friends are people who give you hugs over the phone.

But perhaps the best comforter is someone who is going through the same process, rather than someone who has been through it in the past. Experiences can be shared, and even feelings that might seem unacceptable can be made less shameful by knowing someone else is having them, too. If, of course, they are. One girl who had had a miscarriage found help at a Miscarriage Association group.

Everybody there knew how I felt and I felt that these people were really listening. They understood how I felt when Mother's Day came round and I never had a card. I never had a card on my birthday to Mummy. They understood how I felt towards people who were pregnant and especially to those people who loved to tell you that they had done everything that they shouldn't while pregnant and they had had a healthy baby.

And friends should never underestimate what great relief can come from practical help. You really have to be a psychic super-star not to offend a bereaved person by words; but chores carried out, little tasks performed – no one can possibly misinterpret the kindness behind such practical gestures. But it's important that if help is offered it must be given unconditionally. When one bereaved person was asked if there was anything her friend could do, she asked if she could clean her car. Her friend got very huffy and said she didn't mean anything like that!

Good friends never say: 'If there's anything I could do, let me know.' That's not good enough. A good friend suggests some-thing, or even looks around and sees something that would be useful and just does it. Cooking a meal, shopping, cleaning the house, mowing the lawn, giving a lift in the car, or, often most useful of all, offering to help go through the dead person's personal effects. Deborah Moggach, the partner of the cartoon-ist the late Mel Calman, wrote in *The Times*:

> I love the flowers people send, I love people rushing round. One friend turned up with lunch, vodka and an entire fridgeful of food to pick at when I wanted. One of my sisters slipped in each night and slept in the house, a breathing presence. In the morning she quietly slipped out again.

Jack Tinker, theatre critic of the *Daily Mail*, writing about his daughter who died at twenty-four of drowning during an epilep-tic attack, said:

> Among the literally hundreds of letters was an envelope from one of my most valued friends, the astrologer Patric Walker. Instead of the usual condolences, inside there was a return first-class air ticket to the Greek island where he lives, and the message: 'Come when you need to' written on it.
>
> Eventually I went, and was given that healing peace and seclusion impossible among a family in which each member is having to come to terms with his or her own

personal sorrow. It was only as I was preparing to leave that we even discussed Charlotte's death. And it was then that he gave me the advice I have carried like a talisman ever since, and which I always pass on to parents who have suffered any similar circumstances, though each loss is unique and private. 'Don't look on it as a life interrupted,' said Patric. 'Try to think of it as a life completed and then you can take it with you for the rest of your life.'

And suddenly it seemed to make the first real sense since I had come home on that awful night ... And but for Patric's advice by now I would, I know, be corroded inside by all the If Onlys and By Nows. As it is, for most of the time I have learned to accept hers as a life complete. Looked at like that, I can have no happier last memory. Sometimes, of course, the trick simply doesn't work.

Good things can and do happen. And perhaps it's wrong to criticize other people's many failings, when it comes to dealing with bereaved people, without mentioning how difficult bereaved people themselves can be. Most bereaved people's feelings are chaotic. You never seem to know when they're going to arrive. A friend may turn up for a sympathetic lunch and you don't feel one speck miserable. The minutes she leaves, you burst into tears. Then you probably blame her, quite unreasonably, for not staying long enough. It's all very annoying. The problem is that other people cannot know when you need them unless you tell them. And on the whole the consolation and comfort comes at the time when you need it least – between the death and the funeral, when you have plenty to occupy your mind. It's the same when you have a cold. Just before it you usually feel lousy and no one sympathizes; during the cold when you are sneezing like mad but you usually feel fine, everyone sympathizes, because the symptoms are visible; after the cold, when there are no symptoms but you're feeling drained and weary, equally, no one sympathizes. Similarly, at a time when you are surrounded by obituaries, high drama, undertakers, coffins and so on, you get sympathy by the sackful; but it is after every-thing is over that you really need the comfort. And of course it is then that you have to ask for it – which is always difficult. Sometimes, too, we are confused about our own feelings, so it's small wonder outsiders get even more confused.

I remember talking to a friend after my father died. And I was aware of saying things like: 'I could hardly drag myself out of bed this morning' or 'I felt so miserable the other day' – but it had an awful unconvincing ring about it. Just a sob on the phone would say much more. In my diary I wrote:

> Somehow if I describe how I felt, to Sue, I feel she thinks I'm a fraud. Describing how unhappy one felt yesterday or an hour ago – it's like describing the fish that got away. 'Oh yeah,' you can picture them saying. 'You cried buckets? How many buckets precisely? Sure you cried buckets. You felt sad? How sad exactly? This sad? You can't remember? I put it to you – *did you really feel sad at all?*' And then I wonder myself. Did I feel sad? Or was I just kidding myself?

And yet . . . and yet. We are social animals. We long for the comfort of other human beings. As Blake Morrison wrote:

> I've become a death bore. I embarrass people at dinner parties with my morbidity. I used to think the world divided between those who have children and those who don't; now I think it divides between those who've lost a parent and those whose parents are still alive. Once I made people tell me their labour stories. Now I want to hear their death stories – the heart attacks, the car crashes, the cancers, the morgues. I start to believe that there's such a thing as a 'good' or 'easy' death, just as there is 'good' or 'easy' birth. And I start to write to friends when their fathers die, some-thing I never used to do, something I feel ashamed at not having done before.

I well remember, the night my father died when I was at a party (what was I doing at a party, you may well ask? Well, for some reason it seemed like a good idea at the time, such is the weird way one's mind works during bereavement) someone asked what I had been up to, and I said: 'Well, hey, my father died today. Are your parents alive?' For me, it was a great topic of conversation. I wanted to talk about it all night, all week, all month and, incidentally, all year (and a couple after that, come to that). At that time I didn't want sympathy so much as the chance to compare notes.

Edie's mother wrote movingly about the mourning period after her daughter died of anorexia:

> It is far more complex than personal experience; it is a time of almost primordial communication. We all, without exception, have to face our own death and probably the deaths of some that we love, and for us in the west we tend to bury this fact in the hidden ares of our minds. Then, when a death does occur, especially when it is as shocking as Edie's, all the layers of everyday affairs and concerns are suddenly swept away, and what seemed something shadowy suddenly becomes the only inevitable reality. There is a huge need to acknowledge this thing together, and especially in that particular moment when we have all stopped and witnessed our own vulnerability. I have never before experienced people in such an open state; the barriers were all down. Something else I realized; when a death of such importance occurs, something in one's life has changed and before continuing with other close relationships this must be acknowledged, however briefly; even a word or two. Until that is done there is a sort of blockage in communication.

The bereaved will always want to talk. Most of the time they will always be disappointed. The people they confide in will usually get it wrong, but the bereaved will continue to confide, because even the listeners who get it wrong serve some purpose as people to rage at, innocent parties to blame. But then there will be the odd shaft of light or warm hand to hold, perhaps just briefly, and maybe there will be a moment when you do feel a link with the human race that you had never felt before. In no way does this make the death 'worth it', nor is it any kind of pay-off. But it is an interesting – and not unpleasant – by-product of the death of someone close. How can I put it without sounding as if I'm pushing some kind of irritatingly Pollyanna-ish line on death? It is certainly possible for a bereaved person to get off on this feeling of brief contact. It is, no question about it, better than a slap in the face with a cold fish.

10. Who Am I Now?

I went to the supermarket and looked at the things I'd put in my trolley and I'd bought everything Derek liked. He had peculiar food fetishes, only cherries or only roll mops. I put everything back on the shelves and I wondered, 'What exactly do I like?' I thought I needed psychotherapy because I'd lost track of who I am. I kept asking myself: 'What do I like doing?' Derek didn't like the television on, he didn't like the noise. Perhaps I *do* like television? The frightening thing was I didn't know. I thought I'd lost my bloody mind. (Derek Jarman's friend Keith Collins, quoted in the *Evening Standard* by Pauline Peters after the film director's death from AIDS)

Imagine a picture postcard showing a sunlit bay, blue sea and sky, yellow sand, a grove of green palm-trees, and a red umbrella. Then imagine taking out the colour blue. How would the scene change? Would the sand not look much yellower? And wouldn't the red beachball now become more prominent? Or imagine then removing the tallest palm-tree? How does the group of trees look now? Now another palm-tree is the tallest. Certainly the whole balance of the scene will alter, and all the objects assume different proportions.

When my father died, I felt similarly confused. At one moment it seemed as if a backdrop to my life had changed. And as, if you change a backdrop from a plain white colour, say, to a patterned dark one, so the objects in front change their tones and colours in relation to it, so did I and all the characters in my life alter as well. I saw them differently. Some seemed smaller, some bigger, some further away, some closer, some uglier, some prettier.

At another moment I would imagine my father as a huge, beautiful rhododendron bush that had been growing bigger and bigger in a flower-bed. He was good-looking, extraordinarily clever, well-read, he was a practising artist, he played the piano, he was exceptionally amusing, he had the OBE . . . and he naturally rather overpowered us. As his child, when he died, I couldn't fail to miss him but, also, I could not fail to flourish, too. The rain may have beaten down on me more heavily, but I got more sun, as well.

Others may feel personally diminished by a death. The wives of men who had very strong roles in the community may suddenly realize that they themselves were never any more than creeping vines that collapsed once the stake around which they twisted was removed. Others may find that, amazingly, they still stand strong, without the stake. Their role as the dead person's wife or husband continues to flourish, despite the death of their partner.

Colin Murray Parkes describes a bereaved person as one who must change his internal model of the world to incorporate the new external reality. And this he has to do at a time when he is usually feeling exceptionally miserable and physically low. Feelings of bereavement are bad enough – being stricken with grief, fear, guilt, rage, helplessness, anxiety and shock. But just at this worst moment in your life, you find you've got to redefine yourself as well, something you'd find difficult enough even if you were feeling on top of the world. Shifting sands. As the future looms up uncertain and mysterious, the present has to change as well; and it's no good looking to the past for reassurance either, because with a bereavement the past changes, too.

A phrase that comforters often use is: 'Remember the good times.' When the first person made this hackneyed remark to me, I was, naturally, furious. (Naturally? Remember, anger is almost always the first response to anything, however kindly meant.) The remark implied that we had had bad times – which we had never had. (I later realized that there was a reason we had never had these bad times – they had all been stored up for me to experience after he died; more of that in a moment.)

But death does something to memories. When someone is alive, their present existence seems to withhold the key to the strong-box of remembrance. Why look back when you have them there, in front of you? Your memories are of your last meeting, not the distant past. Close your eyes and think of someone near to you who is alive. How do you imagine them? Probably at the age they are now, in the kind of clothes they are wearing these days, in the house they are living in at present. But when they die, a scrapbook of the past suddenly flies open. Memories come flooding back. When you think of the bereaved person you think of *any* time in their lives, not just the moment you last saw them – when they were small, when you first met, the bad times as well as good times. But death gives access to the past in a way that nothing else can. And this new view of the past sheds new and different light on the present.

At the very same time, while people's death can open up the door to old memories and bring them to life, their deaths also deliver these memories their own death sentence. Not only, when someone dies, does their death bring home to us that the memories are only memories, that those times we had are gone, that the past is past and can never be re-created, but the memories we shared lose their sharpness when there's only one person left to remember them. So when a person dies, one can both find and lose a shared past with them, as well as lose a shared future.

In *More Low Life*, Jeffrey Bernard wrote about the late Frank Blake in 'A Soho Character':

The fact that someone is seventy-four, smokes sixty cigarettes a day and drinks doesn't stop the fact that it's sad when a man dies. You want them to hang on for a little longer . . . Well, there's not many of us left. I was totting up deaths and obituaries the other day and it is rather depressing but inevitable I suppose once you hit fifty. It isn't Soho characters I miss so much as contemporaries. You find yourself looking around and wondering who's next. You avoid the looking glass except for necessities. One of the ways in which I shall miss Frank is that such people are a 'connection'. Not just to life as one is used to it, but to the past and simply being.

Blake Morrison commented, on looking at an old photograph of his father: 'It isn't just (just!) that he is dying. Where he came from is dying too.'

The past dies; the past itself changes. A person may find that when a parent dies they suddenly have access to a lot of resentment and anger that has been thoroughly repressed when they were alive. To come to the realization, after she has died, that your mother did not love you as much as your sister, say, will certainly alter your present. To discover, after your partner has died, that if you could only have brushed aside the resentments, you would have understood how much he loved you, might perhaps make you feel more special now, more lovable, even if more regretful.

And as death releases the dead, it also releases you. At least that's what I felt when my father died. But perhaps I didn't realize what chains of devotion (and I use the word chains advisedly) my father had used to bind me to him. For those with only a faint hold on our own identity, the moment that someone close dies is the moment that you get a vague, vague clue of what it might one day be like to be you. My own father had a reputation in our family for being brilliant – but it is only since he died that I have come to understand that he was only brilliant in certain areas, a head man rather than a heart man. Realizing that a part of him was weak, however, and that he was a human being doing his desperate best, rather than an Artistic and Intellectual Genius who made Midgets of All Around Him, may have resulted in a great deal of rage and confusion for me, but has eventually made my own life slightly more coherent.

I was amused to read a long letter from a friend whose mother had died. He described his intensely affectionate feelings about her, the funeral, the weather on the day of the funeral, every minuscule detail . . . and he ended up, the first time he had ever signed off in this way, 'love from me'. He adored his mother. But within only a matter of months he had married, very late, and soon had a new family. It was as if he could only become himself once his mother had died.

Others may find this freedom to become more themselves a kind of curse. 'I feel all my moral guidance is gone,' said one man. 'I can do what I like now. I hate it.'

Death makes us confront who we are in a most uncomfortable way, particularly if we have been living, as most partners do, partly through, or for, the other. C.S. Lewis was certainly not grateful for the freedom his wife's death gave him. He felt adrift.

I think I am beginning to understand why grief feels like suspense. It comes from the frustration of so many impulses that had become habitual. Thought after thought, feeling after feeling, action after action, had H. for their object. Now their target has gone. I keep on through habit fitting an arrow to the string; then I remember and have to lay the bow down. So many roads lead thought to H. I set out on one of them. But now there's an impassable frontier-post across it. So many roads once; now so many culs de sac.

The late Jill Tweedie wrote of her feelings after the death of her father – a father she feared and disliked.

One minute I was jogging along, snug at the centre of things, and the next I was alone, marooned in a perilous place where I couldn't speak the language or read the words. Where were the travellers who had gone before? Where was the map that would get me out of this icy waste? Or was I to spend the remainder of my life trapped like some iron-age beast in a glacier, mute and immobile, moving inch by inch downhill?

What had happened was that the person I thought of as me had suddenly packed up and gone, like a lover or friend you take for granted and then discover they've been making other plans, finding another place to be, another person to be with and you're stunned and it's too late. I felt it physically, that moment of departure, standing in my father's garden under the pear tree where his deck-chair was still propped. Something shifted inside my skull, did a slippery flip, then slithered away like a fish from a net and I knew it was myself, that fish, off back to the sea. My first sensation was one of relief at being rid at last of some alien growth, the sort people talk about after operations, 'Big as a grapefruit, the doctor said, the size of your fist.' Distress came swiftly after, though, because there was such a void where the fish had been.

I was fine until then, fine right through my forties, thought I'd made it into the harbour. My skin fitted me comfortably, I knew who I was, the good and the bad, and felt secure in my views on everything from religion and politics to the best way of chopping parsley (with scissors, in a mug). For the first time for years money wasn't a problem, I earned enough for my needs and wanted nothing I couldn't buy, or not badly. Work was going well and my children, after the usual alarums and excursions, seemed to me in all essentials satisfactory. It wouldn't be correct to say I looked forward to the future – who looks forward to an ever more tattered ozone layer, dwindling natural resources or, for that matter, their own old age? – but on the whole I considered that the planet and I, having weathered some quite vicious storms in our time, would cope somehow with whatever lay ahead.

Then this mature, confident individual (the ill-natured might say smug) expired overnight along with my father. Nothing remained, not one thought, belief or opinion that I could call mine and hang on to. The smallest decisions were beyond me: my decision-making apparatus had been shot down in flames. I couldn't even judge my own behaviour or the impression I made on others – did I talk too much or not enough? Did the things I said make sense or was I babbling? Were people laughing with me or at me? Had I been right or wrong to react on this or that occasion with anger or placation, indifference or jokes? I had no way of telling. Some virus had attacked my computer and wiped out every disk. Tabula rasa.

The common explanation, a mourning syndrome, a reaction to grief, did not in my case apply. Of that, if of little else, I was sure, despite the cooing of the sentimental and the dogma of shrinks. Parting from my father was neither sweet, sorrowful nor much of a parting. How can you part from someone you've never been with?

Nevertheless it terrified me, the void, the nullity. With no warning I'd lost my grip and gone skeltering back down the well of time to become some primeval organism, a jelly lacking any boundaries, sans any nucleus to speak of, sploshing gloomily about in the primordial soup. From the murk I cried out for my mother, though she, poor thing, had never been much of a lifebelt, being more or less fully engaged in keeping herself afloat.

'Mother,' I cried, 'I'm lost. I'm not myself. I don't who I am any more.'

So who are we now? As the person who has died has become someone else – 'the deceased' – so we have become someone else – 'the bereaved'. Perhaps we are a widow or a widower, where before we were a wife or a husband. Perhaps we are orphans where before we were someone's daughters or sons. When a brother dies, are we still sisters? Or are we only children? If our child has died, can we still call ourselves parents? And what have we lost? We have lost far, far more than just a person. We have lost a shared past, a shared future, possibly a sexual partner, a protector, friend, accountant, cook, driver, audience, scapegoat, fellow-parent, breadwinner, dependant, the bearer of our grandchildren or simply the only person who can set the video timer or remember people's birthdays. We have also *lost the person who we were with that person*. We have lost part of ourselves.

In her diaries, Frances Partridge wrote of how she experienced the change in herself after her husband had died.

> Well, what do I see? Certain things that were always true, others that amount to modifications in my self and my way of life. One of these is that I am, literally, now a different person from the one of 1926–60. When you love and live daily in contact with someone, your two personalities overflow into each other, the dividing barrier is submerged. Part of me was then composed of Ralph's ingredients, just as part of him was of mine. One would think that all growth has stopped by sixty, but like an old gnarled tree trunk one does continue putting out small shoots each year or embracing the barbed wire cutting into one's side.

In later diaries she returned to the same theme.

> Amazed and horrified at the relentless passage of time, the long, white empty lengthening stretch of life without Ralph in it. That's why friends tell the bereaved to *hang on* and the time will pass. It does, all too fast, carrying one further and further away from the only real happiness, before one has the strength even to clasp the painful memory of that happiness close and be sure it never hazes over. I see Ralph shooting off . . . through an infinity of empty space like a star on its orbit, and must submit to his flight. I am astonished by this long blank bit of my solitary life and dread it should be prolonged so that my thirty-five years with him might seem not the whole of my life but a part, in shocking falsity of emphasis.

Someone who has lost a partner may feel that they lose status. A woman who has invested all her time in her partner's career may feel she has not just lost a partner but a role in life. Particularly difficult for the widow is her social life, which can dry up completely after the death of her partner, single women simply not being very popular with hostesses who, naturally, prefer to have single men round their tables. She has changed from a safely married woman to a threat – a merry widow, a black widow, a predatory, scheming woman. People kiss widows differently. Men may hold back in case their affection is misinterpreted. Or they may come closer, hoping that the widow's sexual longing may include them.

Partners miss so much. They miss the social life, the sheer companionship, someone to go to movies with, to concerts, to grumble with, to complain to; they miss the interchange of trivial information, the sharing of interests not really enjoyed by one, but pleasurable for two. Most widows and widowers miss the pleasure of just being able to catch a partner's eye across a dinner table; or the security of going up to their partner at a party and simply being able to stand quietly by, neither alone nor with the group. A widow might once have enjoyed watching football with her husband – but it seems pointless on her own; a widower might have enjoyed hosting dinner parties that he could never conceive of arranging himself. Women can miss just the sheer maleness of having a 'man about the house' – a man to fix the car, to argue doggedly, in a masculine way, to carve the joint, lay the table, do the washing up and all the crazy things that men still seem to do in our society however 'new' they may be. A man may miss the 'femaleness' of a woman. Does he know the difference between coloureds and whites? Wasn't there something about a fluff-catching gadget on the drier he never knew about? Why does the sitting-room never look so pretty now? Was it that she bought flowers? Why don't they look good when he buys them? What is that funny smell? She would surely have known how to get rid of it.

No wonder some men and women hate learning to do the tasks usually done by the opposite sex for themselves. While they remain helpless, some member of the opposite sex in the family will probably pop round and help them out, not so much by helping them fix the lightbulb or darn a sock, but rather giving them a little bit of missing sexuality – 'maleness' or 'femaleness' – that the bereaved partner craves so much. Even if the partner does manage to cope on his or her own, what is their status now? Should the wedding ring still be worn? Would it be wrong to put it away in a drawer? And yet to wear it seems sentimental and anyway might give out the wrong signals to someone new.

Particularly difficult for partners is the reassertion of self, unless they have been very strong as individuals throughout the partnership. Learning to say 'I' instead of 'We' can be a painful task for two people who have grown into each other and become enmeshed. In *Growth Through Loss*, Rosemary Gordon writes about a man who consulted her, complaining that he wished he had been less happy with his wife when she was alive because then he would not be so unhappy now:

> I cannot help but suspect the very happiness he now rues and regrets consisted in large measure of a state of fusion and confusion between the two, this man and his wife, and was preserved at the price of the two being so totally inter-dependent that each of them was only a half person. Thus neither of them alone could, or would, become or remain viable; only the two together could function as a full person and feel themselves to be a full person. This fusion and confusion with the partner-spouse has also most likely iso-lated them or perhaps even alienated each of them from contact with his or her own inner world; and so it may have prevented them from knowledge and experience of the inner world; yet without it neither of them could develop and strengthen trust in the power, benevolence and creativ-ity of their own inner world.

Mary Stott put it powerfully:

> You, who have lived thirty or forty years as half of a pair, go to the pub, or to a women's meeting, or to bingo, or the gramophone society, where most of the people present are half of a pair, and you go home to an empty house. You

are *alone*; you have no one to sound off to, no one to discuss with, no one even to say goodnight to. That's when you begin to know about loneliness. It is ridiculous for people to be lonely, you may say, from the security of your marital partnership, your multitude of friend-producing interests. Little do you know. Death, desertion, disaster at work or in personal life may totally destroy your confidence in yourself.

The practice of suttee in India – in which a widow, having no place in society, is ritually burned after her husband's death – has been virtually wiped out. But some widows in the West – and indeed widowers – often feel that they might as well be thrown on a bonfire, society treats them so shamefully. Small wonder that some widows and widowers carry on at home almost as if nothing has happened, buying sugar for their partner's tea, though they themselves never take it, buying treats for partners unable to appreciate them.

Elspeth Barker, the widow of the poet George, wrote:

I find death utterly unacceptable and I cannot come to terms with it. I can no more conceive of utter extinction, of never, than I can conceive of infinity. I cannot believe that all that passion, wit, eloquence and rage can be deleted by something so vulgar as the heart stopping . . . I am not a widow, I am George's wife. Why must our marriage be nullified by his death? Sons, daughter, aunts, friends all retain their relationship. I shall retain mine.

That's one way of coping. Another is to put the incident – all the love and years of happiness – firmly in the past and look only to the future as if the marriage never took place. Another is to find some kind of niche or shelf in your psychological life where the dead person can exist, leaving room for others if it is needed (which is one of those glib comments that can only be made by those who have successfully achieved such a rearranging of their emotional furniture, and is a useless piece of advice for those who have not yet stumbled across the secret phone number of the emotional furniture remover).

The death of a parent brings us to other new places. Our role in society may be just as secure as it was before, but we suffer our own particular kinds of internal loneliness, and find our interior furniture completely upside down.

Losing a parent means you lose your home and your centre. However much of a home you may have created for your family, in one sense, for you, your own home is always where your parents are. Now that home has gone. The hub of your life has gone. The centre of your life has vanished, and often, feeling only a child inside, you may have to take on the role of family centre yourself.

Unlike the man quoted earlier who felt that with his parents' death all morality had fled, this man found the opposite. 'I never thought anything I did really mattered, because I knew that at home I'd always be accepted and loved, however badly I'd behaved,' he said. 'But now, if I behave badly, where can I go to be accepted? I have, now, to behave well.' One friend said, when his parents died:

> To this very day I regret and hate the sensation of being an orphan. Not an easy word to use when you are fifty but oh, so true. It is cold out front and they did give shelter. Certainly a warmth of the ever-growing catalogue of mutual shared experiences. No longer is there anyone to tell of the idiocies and joys of their grandchildren. And sad not to go through the repetitions of early life, relived again. Ah, a sad business.

As Tony Lake says in his book *Living with Grief*, a parent's death always involves stock-taking. 'Up to now you have led the life which, very largely, others have given you. Now it is yours. You are its sole arbiter. And this fact is itself very important.'

Parents' deaths so often come at a time when our own lives are beset with difficulties. They coincide, usually, with being middle-aged, with going through the menopause, with children leaving home. The deaths come at a time when most of us suddenly realize that we are no longer 'promising', that we can no longer put things off 'until we are grown-up'. We *are* grown-up. Not only that, but we are probably at our very peak, looking forward only to a lessening of physical and mental activity and, eventually, death. Death of a parent also forces us to face up to death. Wake up in the morning and what do you see? Death. Open the door. Death. Answer the phone? Death. It crowds around you, pressing in, whispering: 'I'm here, I'm here, I'm here . . . and I'm coming to get you!'

Death makes us face up to our own mortality. When my father died and I was suddenly parentless, I felt pushed into the firing line. It was as if I'd been sitting in a trench all those years smoking my cigarettes and brewing tea in my billycan while everyone had been out there getting shot, and suddenly my officer had shouted: 'OK, Ironside! Over the top!' Now I was in no-parents'-land with snipers all around. I was next. We have to face the fact that we will die, that we will die alone. We have to face the truth that even with others we basically always are alone, and that unless we give it meaning, life is meaningless.

Blake Morrison wrote of his father: 'Patron and protector, he'd been the wall between me and death; now that wall is gone; now I'm on my own.'

Young children naturally do not find themselves beset with anxiety about mortality when a parent dies. They may, however, be extremely frightened that the remaining parent might die. If you are an older child a death may force you into a new role in the family, playing mum or dad to younger brothers and sisters; if you are a younger brother or sister you may find yourself with a new 'head' of the family, the eldest sibling. You may not like this. Death can force responsibility on to children far beyond their years. In one family, when a hated father died, his son's mother put out his father's clothes the following day. She told her son to put on his dad's clothes and stop going to school. She added: 'Now you're the man of the house.'

Children, however, quite often become compulsive care-givers to younger children, without being told, in order to keep alive the care that they are missing from their parent, albeit they are giving out the care rather than receiving it. Children, of course, often redefine themselves by deciding that they are responsible for their parent's death, weighing themselves down with guilt for the rest of their lives.

And when parents lose children – this is said to be the worst loss of all. Parents lose part of themselves, they lose their children's innocence, they blame themselves because after all a parent's duty is to protect their child from harm, and they lose their genetic future. And those couples who find themselves infertile suffer the added loss of even being parents in the first place. 'Once home from hospital, my mind was a turmoil of outrage,' wrote one woman after a miscarriage ended up with a hysterectomy.

Few people could say anything to help. In desperation I turned to my sister for support but discovered myself adrift in a different world from hers – she has two children. We seemed unable to communicate and without blaming her I recognized my isolation. Left alone, I was over-whelmed by my shame. I was unable to look pregnant women in the eyes, not due to any resentment, but because I was not worthy.

The shock of the possibility of childlessness sent me into a spiral of depression. For months I wept daily. I played mental games with myself; what would I sacrifice for a child? An arm? A leg? The life of a relative? I ticked them all off, knowing that a child was the only thing that would return some meaning to my life. The idea of no children tormented me. Every time I heard of a friend's pregnancy or news of a birth, the yearning felt like a physical pain. I took solace in being bitter and scornful of other, luckier mothers. I accepted that I was now a failed woman. This is what I thought: the female of the species is there to produce the next generation. That is the foundation on which all other successes are built. How can any building stand up without foundation?

An infertile woman turns into an asexual person; a married woman turns into a widow, a threat; a married man turns into a widower, a loner perhaps. A bereaved child may turn into a parent; or find it has a new parent – a brother or sister. A parent who loses an only child loses the role of being a parent and turns back into a childless creature; an adult child who loses its last parent turns into an old, frightened, orphan. And change is threatening not only for us but for those around us. And this change we have to bear on our own, without the support of the person who's died.

Whatever new role we take on, death pushes all of us back on to ourselves. It is a hard, painful business and no wonder, losing someone close, so many people hope that the loved ones are not really gone after all, but are waiting for us. Somewhere.

11. The Spiritual Side

Death is nothing at all – I have only slipped away into the next room. I am I and you are you. Whatever we were to each other that we are still. Call me by my old familiar name, speak to me in the easy way which you always used. Put no difference in your tone; wear no forced air of solemnity or sorrow. Laugh as we always laughed at the little jokes we enjoyed together. Play, smile, think of me, pray for me. Let my name be ever the household word that it always was. Let it be spoken without effort, without the ghost of a shadow on it. Life means all that it ever meant. It is the same as it ever was; there is absolutely unbroken continuity. Why should I be out of mind because I am out of sight? I am but waiting for you for an interval, somewhere very near, just around the corner. All is well. (Canon Henry Scott Holland)

Or is it? Where is 'round the corner'? Where are they now? Have the dead been snuffed out like candles? Or will they be waiting for us on some golden shores when we ourselves die? Are they going to be reincarnated? Or have they joined into a huge spiritual stew from which all of life – plants, animals, birds and fish – is created? There is great need for bereaved people to try to impose some kind of logic or sense on to a situation that I would call a mystery if only the word mystery did not have wonderful and awe-inspiring connotations.

The answer to 'Where are they now?' can only really be supplied by shoulders being shrugged and the statement: 'Yer wha'? *I* dunno.' In other words, we have absolutely no idea at all about where they are.

Being bereaved means asking not just where, but also why. Why, why and why again. And not just why did they die. Why did they die at that particular time? Why didn't someone else, a hopeless crippled vegetable, a loathsome drug-addict, die instead? Why did it happen to me? Why do I have to suffer so much? *Why* did they go? And again, *where* did they go? If bereaved people are not of an accepting nature – and most of us aren't – they can react in one of three ways. They can rage, they can cry, or they can believe that if the dead person is not here, then he must be 'somewhere else'. Certainly when I saw my mother in the chapel of rest, dead, I was quite certain that the thing in the coffin was no way my mother. That was a shell, like a bundle of old clothes. *She wasn't there.* The logical step was to look around for her. Because *she must be somewhere else.* As the saying goes: 'If we still love those we lose, can we altogether lose those we love?'

Do they live on in our hearts, or our families? Certainly there are bits of my father and my mother that I can see in my son. Even bits of my grandmother, although he never knew her. And I don't mean just physical characteristics like a certain smile or a way of walking; I mean an attitude of mind, a cast of joke, a streak of personality.

But if that's not a good enough place for dead souls to live, then the more popular view is that they go to another place, even if that place is in another dimension. The idea is as old as time. (Which does not, of course, mean that it is correct.) The Egyptians put food in dead people's graves to sustain them on their journeys. The language we use for dying often implies that our loved ones have gone to an afterlife – 'passing on', 'departing this life', 'going to heaven'.

Whenever I have written about bereavement I have been showered with utterly charming and utterly sentimental poems, all of which offer consolation by assuring the reader that the dead person is not gone. You will meet again. The relationship you had with the dead person has not stopped. It continues, but just in a different way. As St John Chrysostom wrote: 'For think not, because he is not present, that therefore he is lost; for had he been absent in a foreign land, the title of thy relationship had not gone from thee with his body.' When I asked readers of my problem page to send in poems to comfort the bereaved, the most popular was Canon Henry Scott Holland's prose poem quoted earlier, which begins with the startling statement: 'Death is nothing at all.' And ends with the equally gob-smacking claim that: 'All is well.' (Personally, the word 'bollocks' is the one that springs to my lips after reading that, but that's just a personal view.) But all the other poems and sayings I received were also preoccupied with the denial of death, or rather, to be less judgemental, the idea that death is only part of a process. If 'Death is Nothing at All' was number one in the hit parade of bereaved poems, hot on its heels were these:

> Do not stand at my grave and weep.
> I am not there, I do not sleep.
> I am a thousand winds that blow
> I am the diamond glints on snow
> I am the light on ripened grain
> I am the gentle autumn rain.
> When you awake in morning's hush
> I am the swift uplifting rush
> Of quiet birds in circled flight;
> I am the stars that shine at night.
> Do not stand at my grave and cry.
> I am not there. I did not die.

> I have seen death too often to believe in death.
> It is not an ending but a withdrawal
> As one who has finished a long journey
> Stills the motor,
> Turns off the lights,
> Steps from his car,
> And walks up the path
> To the home that awaits him.

Then there are hundreds of other poems and sayings: 'Remembrance is a golden chain/That links us till we meet again.' 'Life is eternal and love is immortal; and death is only our horizon, and our horizon is nothing save the limits of our sight.' 'They are not lost, our well beloved/Nor have they travelled far/Just stepped inside Home's loveliest room/And left the door ajar.' 'And never, never, be afraid to die/For I am waiting for you in the sky.' 'Though my heart is sad, my soul's aglow/That we'll meet again, I know/I know, I know.'

The trouble is, we don't know. It's a lovely thought. As Amber Lloyd, the founder of the Relaxation for Living Trust, wrote after her husband died:

> For months I woke every morning hoping it was my turn
> . . . I envy people who have the religious conviction of a
> future life together . . . With his Will he left a note saying
> 'We'll meet again, somewhere, sometime' so I cling to the
> hope that we might eventually be joined in some sort of
> togetherness.

But will they? This is the question. We will never know until of course we cop it ourselves. In the meantime some of us have hallucinations to be getting on with, which can be explained away by psychologists as tricks of the mind programmed by habit into seeing people in certain situations. Or it can be argued that these visions are created by the subconscious of the bereaved, so desperate are they for the comfort of some kind of contact with the dead person.

And why not? In *Wuthering Heights*, by Emily Brontë, Heathcliff actually longs to be haunted by Catherine's ghost, rather than be left on his own without her. When he learns of her death, he rages:

> 'Be with me always – take any form – drive me mad! Only
> *do* not leave me in this abyss where I cannot find you! Oh,
> God! it is unutterable! I *cannot* live without my life! I *cannot*
> live without my soul!'
>
> He dashed his head against the knotted trunk; and,
> lifting up his eyes, howled, not like a man, but like a savage
> beast getting goaded to death with knives and spears.

The people who are lucky enough to experience hallucinatory visitations would, I am sure, deny that they were figments of their imagination. And there is no reason to suppose they are, despite the sensible reasoning of brain experts. I have had only one hallucination in my life and for me it was more real than anything I've encountered in 'real' life.

Actor William Roache, talking to Danny Danziger in the *Independent*, spoke of his feelings after his daughter Edwina died at eighteen months.

I tried to pull myself together to ring my mother, but as soon as I tried to talk I burst into tears. I didn't want to go out, I didn't want to see anybody. We just talked and talked, myself and Sara. We talked for four days and the funeral was getting near, and I honestly didn't think I could get through it. But on the morning of the funeral I woke up – and I know I was awake, it wasn't a dream – and I had a vision in which I saw this halo of shining gold, with Edwina's face absolutely clear in the middle, smiling down. And I felt a release as this great glow of light poured into me. At the same time there was this sense of peace and tranquillity. And the grief went, not totally, because there's still an element, but from then on I was able to cope.

Hallucinations are most common during the first ten years of a bereavement and older people seem to experience them more often. Some see the dead person, but some smell them and a small percentage have felt touched by them. Certainly most bereaved people have 'seen' the dead person out of the corner of an eye getting on to a bus, vanishing round a corner, sitting on a park bench. And how difficult it is to explain these sightings to other people without being thought completely crazy.

Georgina Monckton movingly described a spiritual experience that came to her a few months after her small daughter's death.

The feeling of pain was almost too much to bear. All I wanted was to be with Isobel. One day I was ironing. I was on my own, distraught because no one understood how low I was feeling. Suddenly I had the extraordinary sensation that Isobel was in the room. I thought I could hear her saying: 'Come to me.' I could feel the pull of her presence. Looking back, I'm sure she was saying: 'I'm here. You're going to be all right. I'm with you.' But because I was so grief-stricken and couldn't think logically, all I felt at that moment was Isobel pulling me to her – one way and one way only. It was like tunnel vision.

What also comforted her was a dream, after the anniversary of her daughter's death.

Isobel was lying horizontally, her body rock-hard; dead, colourless, grey, just as I remembered her in her coffin. Yet her face was alive. She was saying: 'Mum, look at me. Here are my arms, they're dead and hard. My legs are the same, my tummy's the same. Now look at my face.' It was full of expression. She looked peaceful, but still alive. Her face was saying: 'I'm still alive, my spirit is alive. I can see you and I'm with you all the time, don't worry.' I woke up feeling comfortable and peaceful; everything crystal clear. In my mind Isobel has gone to a very special place . . . she will be with us, as a family, forever.

Another mother was comforted by a different kind of experience. Twelve hours before her son died in a motorcycle accident, she was sitting alone in her living-room and all around where she sat there was the most indescribable exotic sweet scent.

I can only describe it as flowers, but I've never smelt flowers like this. Why should I have smelt that fragrance about twelve hours before he died? He was killed on his way home at 6.30 a.m. the following morning. I also had a brief smell of the same aromatic sweetness about two days after his death, but that only lasted for a minute or two.

The strangely sweet smell is recorded by quite a few bereaved people – the scent is described as being like hyacinths or lilies. Sometimes these feelings of someone's presence linger long after the person has died. Some people seem to carry the feeling of their loved one with them for ever. Actor George Baker said in the *Daily Mail*:

> All my life I've felt his [my father's] presence. Years after he died I was on the number 73 bus going past the Royal Albert Hall in London. In my mind my dad was sitting next to me and we were having a really good chat. Another passenger came up the stairs and I only just stopped myself remarking: 'Sorry, that seat is already taken.'

Jayne Zito, whose husband, Jon, was murdered by a schizophrenic, had the same experience. She said in the *Daily Mail*:

> When people talk about bereavement they often say they have the feeling that their loved ones have gone. But I don't feel that. My counsellor says I've developed my own religion called Jonism. I honestly believe he's all right. I believe that he hasn't gone far. Just after he died I would sit really still. I thought if I was completely motionless I'd be able to feel him. Sometimes I would almost sense him when I came home or I would hear him coming through the front door. I think Jon is always going to be on my mind, he's always going to be part of me.

It's interesting that she refers to her feelings as religious, because Professor Isaac Marks, in *Living with Fear*, described a man who, when his father died, 'looked into his eyes and as he stared at me something happened to us. As if something had gone into me. I felt all warm inside. I'm not interested in this world any longer. It's a sort of religious feeling. I feel as big as a house. I fill the room.' Contact with the dead can feel like a spiritual experience in itself. 'We did not merely love one another. We *were* each other. How could she not be there?' wrote Lawrence Whistler after his wife's death. And astrologer Jonathan Cainer, interviewed in *Hello*, talked about his late wife, who died in a car crash:

We always did get on – we were deeply in love and in a curious way I now feel our relationship is safe for ever, which brings me great joy. The fact that she's no longer here doesn't detract from the impact she makes. At times when there's something special going on with the kids, I send her a psychic snapshot; as if to say, 'Look, you'll be pleased with this.' I'm blowed if I'm going to let a small matter like death get in the way of our relationship.

Not everyone has these experiences on their own, however, but they so long for some 'evidence' that their loved one lives on that they visit mediums who, though to an outsider they may seem to provide often very mundane information, can be incredibly reassuring to those who visit.

Visiting mediums is a somewhat dodgy business because they are popularly perceived as charlatans. Any medium who gets a few facts right is usually accused, behind his back, of looking up the husband's obituary, say, in the local paper, and regurgitating it to a gullible widow. At worst they are seen to be hand in hand with the devil. For some reason it is fine to believe in reincarnation, or to believe in eternal life in heaven, but medium-visiting is regarded as rather sick, shabby and stupid.

Perhaps just as many people turn from the church and God after a bereavement as turn to God and mediums. But do they turn to mediums because death opens a curtain on a real existence, an existence, perhaps, that runs alongside the experience of daily life – a true 'other' world? Or do people go to mediums out of fear, because they are so unprepared to accept the very awfulness and betrayal of death, life's sting in the tail, that the immortality offered by spiritualism anaesthetizes some of the pain of dealing with the true horror of death? I have no idea – I have been equally convinced by each idea, and equally unconvinced, when reflecting in other more, or less, cynical moments, too.

Needless to say, C. S. Lewis has harsh words on the subject.

He was certain there was no afterlife of the kind we popularly imagine.

'Upon the further shore', pictured in entirely earthly terms ... Reality never repeats. The exact same thing is never taken away and given back. How well the Spiritualists bait their hook! 'Things on this side are not so different after all.' There are cigars in Heaven. For that is what we should all like. The happy past restored.

Later he wrote: 'What pitiable cant to say "She will live for ever in my memory." Live. That is exactly what she won't do.' And another angry explosion: 'How do they know she is "at rest"? Why should the separation (if nothing else) which so agonizes the lover who is left behind be painless to the lover who departs?'

When a friend died, he felt a certainty about his continued life, but 'I have begged to be given even one hundredth part of the same assurance about H. [his wife]. There is no answer. Only the locked door, the iron curtain, the vacuum, absolute zero.'

Recalling the night after his mother's death Toby Young wrote:

That evening we held an informal gathering for some of her friends. It should have been a touching occasion, but I found myself becoming increasingly irritated. It was held in my mother and father's bedroom with her body still lying there. Several of them said they could feel her spirit in the room. I thought: you sentimental fools, she's dead, what are you talking about? It felt like they were inventing an afterlife for her because they couldn't bear the thought that she was gone for ever, extinct. But of course they were perfectly entitled to play whatever tricks they wanted to avoid this appalling thought. It was me who was being odd by insisting on being unsentimental.

Lawrence Whistler felt just as bitter as he talked of his revulsion at the idea of visiting a spiritualist after his wife died. 'A spiritualistic lady soon offered to "put us in touch", delivering, by way of sample, a "message" from Jill so banal as to suggest that her personality had been dissolved rather than preserved. It repelled me.'

There is another strong argument, not so much about whether you see the loved one again, but about what good it does you. True, some people feel fantastically reassured that their loved ones aren't gone for ever. But why should knowing you're going to see them again be any great comfort? They are not here today. Or tomorrow. Or next year. Depending on how old you are, it could be years and years before you ever see them again. Even if they had emigrated to Australia you could visit them, and telephone. But you would still miss them desperately. Knowing, or believing, that you will you see your loved one again one day in the far distant future is not going to alleviate the pain of living without them in the present.

But this girl, who had suffered a miscarriage, got comfort.

I was in such a state as to what to do that last night I visited a psychic fair and had a reading from a medium. She picked up on so many things that she could not have guessed at, and she herself had been through the misery of repeated miscarriages and the death of a baby only half an hour old. She told me that the spirits of babies who are miscarried go to a higher place and she herself had seen her children in spirit. In some strange way this comforted me a lot.

Despite the obvious comfort that visiting mediums and spiritu-alists can offer, the church is firmly anti-spiritualism, many vicars believing it to be the handiwork of the Devil. Even when they don't go that far, they are extremely wary. But if it comforts the bereaved, does it really matter whether it is true in the church's book or not? It helps, it makes people feel warm and loving, it harms no one. Don't knock it. But knock it, of course, they do. On an *Everyman* programme in 1994, Bernard Cartright, Director of Churches for Health and Healing, said:

I think for someone who has been bereaved to go to a spiritualist church is somehow interfering with the very natural grief process. We know that grief follows a particular pattern although it's not the same with every person. But to try to make contact with the dead militates against a genuine quest for peace.

In the same programme Canon Dominic Walker OGS, co-chairman of the Christian Deliverance Study Group, gave a similar doom-and-gloom message:

I can remember a mother who had lost her five-year-old child and she went along to a spiritualist church and she kept getting messages so she believed from this boy and most of the things were things that he said, toys that he played with and she kept going and she went on going week after week and she didn't go through the natural grieving process and then a year later she had a major breakdown and it really was the fact that she hadn't learnt to let go and she hadn't really coped with any of the grieving process which involves asking why, why me, why does this happen, feeling guilt, anger, all these things she'd bottled up and in the end she had a breakdown and ended up in a psychiatric hospital.

(I just love the way these clergymen talk so glibly about the 'natural grief process' and bang on about 'stages'! If only it were so simple!)

But it is not just mediums and spiritualists who can sometimes convince the bereaved that there is an eternal life and prevent them from accepting the fact of a loved one's death. The church itself with all its talk of resurrection, and its confusing messages about Christ being risen and born again, is also responsible for a lot of angst along the lines of: 'Are they dead?' 'Will we meet again?' 'Are they in heaven?' 'Are they in hell?' 'Have they really gone?' and so on.

Had the bereaved woman in Canon Walker's story consulted

her parish priest she might have been fed the line peddled by my local vicar. She would have been told that death is a joyful thing, the gateway to eternal bliss and joy. 'Hopefully one's sadness will be mingled with a great relief to know the departed is experiencing eternal life . . . Jesus promised the thief he would be welcomed into paradise, where we grow in holiness, and continue an eternal search for God which will never end . . . Death is the greatest gift that God can give us . . . "Dead", "death", "died" – use these words as the key for the magnificent gifts that await us!'

In 1 Corinthians 15, 22 she could have read: 'As in Adam all die, so also in Christ shall all be made alive.' She would still have believed her son was somewhere, waiting for her. The truth is none of us knows what happens when people die. But that truth is very important. It is essential for those of us who do not have a strong belief in the spirit world, or some kind of reincarnation or afterlife, to be truthful about our doubts and muddles, to ourselves, to our friends, and to children. When children ask us, 'Where has Daddy gone?' adults should be honest. To tell a child that a close relative has gone to heaven to be with Jesus is a useless piece of information. It means no more than that they have gone to Manchester to see a man about a dog. Heaven is a tricky enough concept for us adults – not to mention Jesus, about whom millions wonder whether he was the son of God.

'My whole world was empty and black without her,' said one adolescent girl whose mother had died, quoted by Jill Krementz. 'I wanted her back but they kept saying how grateful we must be now she was with Our Lord and not suffering any more. I felt so selfish because I wanted her so much and I knew I shouldn't – that that was bad and selfish.'

Certainly if anyone says anything about God taking a close relative away, the child is going to have very strong feelings that God is bad. In an old Cruse publication, *When Children Grieve*, Alfred Torrie wrote:

If parents say the parent has gone to God or to Jesus, the

child then has another problem. 'Only a bad God would take the father' so this way we destroy his idea of God as good. It would be safer to say that death is the end of life or the absence of life. They say the surest way to destroy a child's faith is to tell him God has taken from him the one he loves and to frighten him by talk of an ill-defined place where everyone goes after death.

He recommends putting it like this:

> You see darling, before you came to me to be born you were a spirit and we gave you a body to put on like a dress. Dresses don't last and Great Grandma had worn hers out and didn't want it any more so now she's gone back to being a spirit. Now she's free of all her aches and pains and not old any more.

Torrie's heart was in the right place, but were I his granddaughter, his bizarre description would ensure that in future I would dread the sight of every hole in my jumper. But to explain to a child this difference between flesh and spirit is hard, without using potentially alarming similes. Perhaps they might start to see the point if they were quoted J. B. Priestley, who remarked that no one says, 'He is a body.' It is always 'He has a body.'

Wondering about what this 'he' consists of, bodyless, what is this essence within not only the clothes but the flesh and the bones, pushes anyone who is half-way reflective into considering what is the essence that lies within themselves. This introspection, which may result in a better understanding of who and what we are, is the only painful pay-off of bereavement.

12. Is There a Pay-off?

> The open confrontation of the loss of a loved one, and of the grief that follows it, can be an enriching experience . . . (Rosamond Richardson, *Talking about Bereavement*)

What utter nonsense! There is a school of thought that will not countenance the idea that death is simply a horrible, vile experience that usually brings only sadness, guilt, anger and pain in its wake. That's only part of the story, it is claimed. Every cloud has a silver lining. And when it comes to bereavement, this lining is usually presented as some kind of enrichment. While there may be some argument for death making the scales fall from our eyes, the idea that it is enriching is, I believe, only another piece of false comfort, a euphemism for finding out more about the harsh reality of life, and a euphemism every bit as icky as phrases like 'passing the great divide' or 'losing' instead of 'dying'.

The attitude is informed by the tyranny of positive thinking – the same sort of tyranny that obliges AIDS victims to twist their brains into thinking of themselves as People Living with AIDS rather than people dying of AIDS – and it is the last kind of attitude that you want forced on you when you're bereaved. It is bad enough being told – if not literally, then obliquely – that you ought to be mourning when you are dealing with a lot of other far more complicated feelings than mere grief; but then to be told by someone with a saintly smile on his face that death brings with it its own rewards is, simply, cruel. While it might be absolutely true to say that some people came through the Nazi concentration camps wiser and better human beings, that statement is shocking and offensive if it isn't qualified by a detailed description of the atrocities committed inside. It is also a shocking statement if it isn't qualified by the fact that some people died there and some people's spirits were broken by the camps as well, and some people's trust in human and spiritual nature never, ever, returned. It is in fact pretty shocking said at all unless it is said by someone, about themselves, who has actually been through the experience.

Listen, for instance, to Susan Poidevin in *Coming Through*:

> Bereavement sets an intellectual challenge ... It is possible to come through the spiritual crisis of bereavement to find a new meaning and purpose in life ... Bereavement is a challenge to make the most of our lives and relationships with each other, and to mature from a stressful experience with more compassion, self-knowledge, depth of feeling and character, and with more to give to those who need us.

In *The Courage to Grieve*, Judy Tatelbaum writes: 'Just as whole forests burn to the ground and eventually grow anew, just as spring follows winter, so it is nature's way that through it all, whatever we suffer, we can keep on growing.' Another writer said: 'There is no growth without pain and conflict; there is no loss which cannot lead to gain.' Anyone who has been bereaved knows what they are trying to say. But it is terribly important to say it properly, so that it will not be misunderstood. And it is important, when it's said, that it's meant properly, too. I certainly remember writing in that same kind of gloopy 'growth and death' vein about six months after my father died, and it is only now that I realize that it was all yet another kind of dishonesty I used, to kid myself into comfort. As Beverley Raphael says in *The Anatomy of Bereavement*, a handbook for the caring professions, it is terribly easy to agree that 'in the darkness of death lies mystery and romance as well'. It is such an attractive idea. It makes us attractive, too, as we saw earlier. But it's a fantasy – grief and suffering seen through rose-coloured spectacles.

Of course there's no reason why we shouldn't find pleasure in the fact that we have been in touch with the mysterious and romantic. But those two areas are not the only ones we have touched, if indeed, we have really touched them at all. We have actually been in touch with incredible and uncomfortable pain and we have probably gone through it and are going through it and will continue to go through it with feelings of greed, rage, sadness, misery and hatred. We *call* it being in touch with the mysterious in the same way as a salesman calls his worthless product magical or exciting. But the only growth or knowledge comes not in imagining that the ropy old vacuum cleaner he flogged us actually does pick up more than the old one; nor in the disappointment that it doesn't pick up fluff any better than the old one – rather less, in fact. The growth comes from realizing that you were sold a pup, and that door-to-door salesmen generally sell you pups. That there are people like that out there. That this is human nature. *This is what life is like.* This knowledge, that people can be deceptive, that cruel death comes, this is what is interesting and makes us wiser than people who haven't been through the experience.

Barbara Ward, in *Healing Grief,* wrote: 'Grief is like a butterfly cramped up in a cocoon. Once it breaks out of its confining shell it opens to the light and is transformed.' No, no, no. Grief may be like a butterfly cramped up in a cocoon. But it never flies away, beautiful and colourful, full of life. If it does emerge, it is as a slimy, black, poisonous beetle. Grief and bereavement are miserable, miserable emotions. Leave them as they are, real and raw, because that is where the truth comes from. Don't distort reality by transforming grief into a butterfly.

Even more irritating, perhaps, is Edith Sitwell in her poem 'Eurydice':

> Love is not changed by death
> And nothing is lost and all in the end is harvest.

But it's not harvest. Or if it is, most bereaved people would look at their crop and compare it to a row of shrivelled-up broad beans thick with black-fly, or a heap of hard green tomatoes, or bolted celery. The harvest of bereavement isn't sheaves of golden corn brought in by buxom country girls with songs on their lips and mystery and romance in their eyes. The harvest of bereavement is simply the knowledge that there is no harvest, that your seeds don't grow, they die.

The idea that death is enriching is a myth, every bit as evil as telling a child packed off to a horrible boarding school that 'Everything will be all right when you get there.' It is a false promise, and encourages the bereaved to live in hopes of a golden globule of fulfilment that will come their way if they wait and wait for the 'blessing' that comes to those who mourn. If a horrible person who was a burden to you all your life died, your life might indeed be enriched by his absence. But if someone you love dies, you are not enriched, you are only enlightened. And the light may not be the warm glow from a pink-stained forty-watt bulb in a cosy drawing-room; it may be the harsh eye-watering ray from a neon strip in a rain-lashed roadside café.

Yet even gurus of death, like Elizabeth Kubler-Ross, argue that death has a purpose, that it is a kind of present from God. 'You will not grow if you sit in a beautiful flower garden, and somebody brings you gorgeous food on a silver platter,' she wrote. 'But you will grow if you are sick, if you are in pain, if you experience losses, and if you do not put your head in the sand, but take the pain and learn to accept it, not as a curse or punishment, but as a gift to you with a very, very specific purpose.'

Some gift. A subscription to *Child Abusers Weekly* would be more acceptable to most of us than the 'gift' of death. However. However. There is a pay-off. The pay-off is in information. Death happens. It will happen to all of us. It is quite often an agonizingly painful experience for those who are left behind. It is part of life. Life includes death for everyone. The death of someone close hammers this information into our heads like a masonry nail. Those who have experienced bereavement have a clearer idea of what life is about than those who have not.

A widow said she looked at life after bereavement in a completely different way. 'I look at a crowd and I think: "You just don't have a clue. You're going to die and you've no awareness of it at all. Your life is such a small space in time and yet you don't think anything about it."'

Now how we interpret the information we have gained is entirely up to us as individuals. The realization of something of what life is actually about is just as likely to produce a completely cynical reaction as a feeling of wonder. Writing in *The Times*, for instance, Celia Haddon gave a harrowing description of her mother's death. The process took seven days and she died in a way that Celia says she could never have permitted for a dog or a cat. She wrote that at the end, her mother's breath was

> so foul, that I could not sit close to her without wanting to throw up . . . One of her ears now had red blotches from the pressure of the pillow. One of the blotches was turning black. She was rotting. She looked like one of those prehistoric men that are found in bogs. The individual features of the flesh were being suspended by the impersonal skull. Her eyes were by now half open, but unseeing . . . I sang her a hymn and told her how much I loved her . . .

When her mother finally died, she reflected:

> But should we not have spared her the last seven days of physical decay and distress? Her dying was a surprise, a shock. Perhaps her suffering death will bring me to a new spiritual insight in time, but at the moment it lies like a great bleak shadow on each new day of my life.

And a young man whose partner died of AIDS:

> My own feeling is that yes, I have learned something. I have learned that life is incredibly cruel. I just hope there isn't an afterlife because if there is I have no doubt more tortures are dreamt up for us there. Life, or afterlife, *nein danke*. Not after what I've been through.

My widower friend, who did not find the death of his wife remotely enriching, wrote:

Cruse has sent me some more pamphlets, including their newsletter, *Chronicle*. It contains a couple of articles by widowers and a list of books published by bereaved, but they served to emphasize that every case is unique to the person bereaved. My own experience would be no help to anyone else if I wrote it, because theirs would be not quite the same. None of the articles are about the very old who are left alone after many, many years of marriage, it isn't realistic to speak of starting a new life, of trying to get something out of new possibilities such as travel, because the chances are you won't feel well enough. The difference between having children and not is enormously important as well; there is nobody to whom I come first.

On the other hand, contact with death can, by giving less sense to our everyday lives, make more sense of a spiritual one. 'I believe the way to peace is not to mourn, but to free her in your mind and heart and realize she is always whole, always real because she is spiritual – and *so are you*,' wrote Joyce Grenfell to a friend on hearing of the death of another.

We don't become spiritual *when* we die. We have always been spiritual and that, as I see it, is what life is for – to discover and rejoice in this. It leads into harmonious living *now*. It reveals what is actually *real* and *durable*.

Iris Murdoch writes in similar vein:

In many cases something good can be retained or learnt from the experience of emptiness and non-being [as a result of facing bereavement]. Should it not be taken as a spiritual icon or subject for meditation? There is nothing that cannot be broken or taken from us. Ultimately we are nothing. A reminder of our mortality, a recognition of contingency, must at least make us humble. Are we not then close to the deep mystery of being human? When we find our ordinary pursuits trivial and senseless are we not right to do so? The experience of emptiness may be a shock soon forgotten, or a lifelong reminder, a moral inspiration, even a liberation, a kind of joy.

I'm not so sure about joy, but liberation perhaps, yes. We gain liberation from lies. The experience of death and bereavement is, there is no doubt, bitterly enlightening. It forces those left to confront the fact that life *is* a bed of roses – consisting mainly of thorns.

Perhaps we can realize that we are all mortal and if we are to enjoy life we must live for the moment. 'Life is a preparation for the fullest enjoyment of the next minute; but to be aware of death is to appreciate the never-to-come-again worth of that minute, free of the dark,' wrote Christopher Leach, in *Letters to a Younger Son*.

Albert Schweitzer advocated dwelling constantly on the topic of death in order to enjoy life more:

We must all become familiar with the thought of death if we want to grow into really good people. We need not think of it every day or every hour. But when the path of life leads us to some vantage point where the scene around us fades away and we contemplate the distant view right to the end, let us not close our eyes. Let us pause for a moment, look at the distant view, and then carry on. Thinking about death in this way produces love for life. When we are familiar with death, we accept each week, each day, as a gift. Only if we are able thus to accept life – bit by bit – does it become precious.

The mother of Edie, the anorexic who died, wrote:

I feel empathy with a whole aspect of human experience. Whatever life is all about we don't have an inalienable right to happiness. Suffering is just as much a part of living as joy. To live wholly, we must use everything that happens, good and bad, bend with it, flow with it, learn from it, and try to tackle each day as it comes, knowing that there is a time limit for us all and it may not be long.

The fact that we can look at death as a harsh reality makes it far less frightening. Sometimes death can, anyway, free us of some unpleasant person in our lives, or from the hindering trait of someone we love. It can make us aware of some of our good points. While it can bring out the worst in some, it can also bring out the best in others. Many is the family that has been reconciled, or which has reaffirmed affectionate feelings unspoken through laziness. 'After my father died I had the most wonderful conversation with my brother,' said one woman. 'We have not talked like that for over twenty years. It made me feel so warm and close to him, it was like rediscovering something I had lost.'

Bereavement means loss, but loss can mean freedom of one kind or another. With the death of someone close, old barnacles are scraped off the bottom of our boats; their absences may reveal the odd crack where the water leaks in, but they lighten us, and the hideous experience of our own mortality does give us the chance to reassess our lives and do something with them. Susan Ardill wrote in *Death of a Mother*:

> The relief I felt at her death was, of course, deeply ambivalent. Yet there it was, undoubtedly real. That she died when she did has enabled me to at least try and change how I am in the world. In that sense I feel it's quite lucky for me that she died while I was relatively young, that I got my chance early in my life. Now it's not her death I have to worry over, but what went before it and continues from it.

The realization that we are, in the end, alone, that we are free of partner or family, that we can do whatever we want, can be both liberating and frightening at the same time. It is like being a budgie in a cage on a window-sill and finding that someone has left the door open. No, we may not have particularly enjoyed life in our cage, but we are used to it. Now we have a decision to make. We can cower in a corner, as far from the open door as possible; we can sit nervously just by the open door, admiring the view without the bars and imagining what it might be like outside; or we can attempt a first tentative flutter. Outside there is sun, rain, and leafy trees; outside are predatory birds, cats, too. Where do we find our food? Where do we want to fly to? Given, by bereavement, the opportunity to be ourselves and having the chance of starting a second time around, what are those ambitions that we always vaguely hoped one day we could pursue? Hiding in grief or resentment about a death may be one way of resisting facing up to our creative selves.

At least we see the truth more clearly. It may not be a truth that is particular pleasant and some may find it vile, but it is true. But on second thoughts can truth be pleasant or vile? Probably not. It's just true. Which is exactly why the idea that it is enriching or gift-like is so false. Death is not a gift, it is not a harvest, nor does it enrich. However, it certainly teaches us a lesson.

I have a son. As a mother I want him to have experiences that will help him to mature, both emotionally and spiritually. Recently he said: 'I hope you don't think I'm being rude, Mum, but I do hope that when you die I'll experience your death in the same way as you've experienced grandpa dying. I know it's been terrible, but you do seem,' he added, rather nervously, 'to have found it extremely interesting as well as sad.' Well, it was absolutely terrible, actually. But it *was* also interesting. And I hope he experiences my death in the same way, too. Without wishing to pop off quite yet, I hope I die young enough for him to experience what it is like to live without parents for a good part of his life. That he will be able to know what death is like so that he, like me, has a chance to get his priorities sorted out before he is too old. So that he, like everyone who suffers a bereavement, gets a *chance* to see what life is *really* like. He may find that death drives him to church or to suicide; to become cynical; to love the present more; to become depressed; to become more his own man; to realize that he can actually do without me, in reality, not in imagination. He may find life sweeter; he may find life crueller. Whatever, and however, he lives life, it will almost certainly be truer.

As Tolstoy wrote in *Anna Karenina*, when he described Levin's feelings on confronting his brother's death:

Death, the inevitable end of everything, confronted him for the first time with irresistible force. And death, which was here in this beloved brother who groaned in his sleep and from force of habit invoked without distinction both God and the devil, was not so remote as it had hitherto seemed to him. He felt it in himself too. If not today, then tomorrow! If not tomorrow, then in thirty years' time – wasn't it all the same? And what this inevitable death was, he not only did not know, not only had never considered, but could not and dared not consider. 'Here I am working, wanting to accomplish something, and completely forgetting it must all end – that there is such a thing as death.'

He sat up in bed in the dark, crouched and hugging his knees, holding his breath from strain as he thought. But the more mental effort he made, the clearer it became to him that it was indubitably so, that in looking upon life he had indeed forgotten one little fact – that death comes and puts an end to everything, that nothing was even worth beginning and that there was no help for it. Yes, it was awful, but it was so.

13. Final Thoughts

And a ship without a rudder may wander aimlessly among perilous isles yet sink not to the bottom. (Kahlil Gibran in *The Prophet*)

I have agonized long and hard over this final chapter and found it particularly difficult to get down to. Why? Many reasons. Originally I had given it the title 'Help' and found that I shrank like an animal from the very word. It just sounds such a stupid, empty little word in the face of something as big as bereavement. 'HELP!' perhaps, as in a shriek from a terrified victim. But 'Help' as in sensible advice and giving it – I can feel my heart start to race, see the hairs rise on my wrist. Help? Help? There *is* no help. There is just pain, emptiness and time. It really is important, for those who look for the truth, at least, that this feeling of helplessness is properly acknowledged. It is only then that sympathy, and tips and coping strategies can be properly received – not as cures for what is a chronic, incurable illness, but as dabs of comfort, cold flannels on the sweating brow, in the time when the illness rages the worst.

Comfort? There is none really, but when you are in agony or confusion, it is nice to have friends on the sidelines wringing their hands and saying: 'Poor you. I wish I could do something.' It is good to have friendly nurses around your bed of bereavement, but they can really do nothing but hold your hand.

Advice? True, the bereaved usually throw it back in the face of the giver, but there are some tips and ideas about ways of passing the time and perhaps distracting yourself while you sit tight, waiting for the reverberations of bereavement to ring less loudly in your ears.

Drugs? The bereaved may be offered sleeping tablets or tranquillizers by the doctor. It's worth accepting them, remembering that *you don't have to take them*. You might take them, you might not. It's up to you. There's no question that if you wake night after night, racked with the kind of agonizing pain and despair that certain bereavements bring, one or two nights knocked for six by drugs is no bad thing. Never feel guilty for taking them; never feel guilty for not taking them. Edie's mother wrote:

> Looking back over the time of my most acute grief, I feel strongly that it would have been very negative, even destructive, for me to have taken any tranquillizer or drug which might have dulled my perceptions and awareness. Just as nature has developed a very ecological balance, which a few thoughtless acts can upset, so I felt my body had its own physical and biochemical way of dealing with grief, and it dictated the right reactions at the right time. I do feel that if I had been fuzzy with pills certain issues would have been delayed and I would have had to deal with them at the wrong time, for other people as well as myself. There wouldn't have been that 'one-ness' in shock. I wanted to be fully aware at the death of my kid, just as I was at her birth.

But you are not that mother. Maybe you do want to take pills now and again. If taking pills means that you're not physically debilitated by lack of sleep and anxiety, then you might just be able to cope with a little more strength than if you hadn't had chemical help. But, of course, if you're offered anti-depressants as opposed to barbiturates or tranquillizers, you must certainly not take them casually. It's essential that you follow the doctor's instructions and take them consistently unless you suffer unacceptable side-effects, in which case you should see your doctor again.

Distractions? Taking a holiday is the most obvious distraction, and many bereaved people feel a great sense of relief being away from the scene. But others feel they are just running away from facing something they should be facing. And travel can be very lonely when you're miserable. Which is worse? To be slumped in despair and depression on a cold and rainy night at home, on a day when the sky has been green with menace, or to feel despairing and depressed on a glorious beach abroad, miles from anyone you know really well, and surrounded by happy young couples, with nothing but an empty house full of memories to look forward to on your return? Travel can make the toughest of us feel vulnerable and powerless, too. Jeremy Howe, whose wife, Dr Elizabeth Howe, was murdered, tried going away by himself but it was a bad idea. 'I clearly hadn't given myself time to unwind and subconsciously it was deliberate. I wasn't at work, I wasn't with the children. I didn't feel real.'

Counselling? If your bereavement film gets stuck on constant replay, bereavement counselling can help to jerk you out of either deep depression or obsessive thinking – usually of the 'if only' variety. He or she can't get you through the black tunnel, but can yell directions from the other end. If your feeling is, 'What's the point of seeing one?' ask yourself, 'What's the point of not seeing one?' The worst that can happen is that you have successfully killed a whole hour of bereavement time; the best is that you get some nugget of consolation or wisdom. But make sure you see a counsellor who is sympathetic. If necessary, shop around if you can possibly face it. Some have been known to bang on about their own bereavement, and one woman who lost a child was horrified to find the counsellor's room stuffed with pictures of her own family. The counsellor asked her to hug her inner child, when the only child she wanted to hug was the one she had lost.

Children really can benefit from seeing a counsellor who's not involved in any way with the dead person. Some people think that children may be too young to understand about death. Sadly, they are not too young to misunderstand. And talking to someone with whom they don't have to pick their words can be incredibly helpful. If Dad has died and Mum is beside herself with grief, how can a child ever express to her that part of her is pleased he's gone, or perhaps that he feels guilty that it was his bad behaviour that made the parent die, for instance, without causing lifelong offence?

Another way of passing the bereavement time is to talk to the dead person as if they were there. In Judy Tatelbaum's *Courage to*

Grieve, she suggests putting the dead person in a chair and speaking to them, telling them why you miss them, why you loved them (or not), why you're pissed off (or thrilled) with them for not being around any more, and, naturally, the things you wish you'd said to them before they died. In her workshops she then encourages her clients to get into the vacant chair and become the dead person themselves, replying to what they've said. One boy became his mother and told himself that he loved him; a wife became her dead husband and gave herself permission to get rid of his things and start a new life.

Another way of keeping the hurt down to the minimum is to continue with every old habit that you can possibly maintain on your own. One widow gave herself a 'husband present' on her birthday to comfort herself, and wrote:

The evenings were the hardest to bear. The ritual of the hot drink, the lumps of sugar for the two dogs, the saying of prayers – his boyhood habit carried on throughout our married life – the goodnight kiss. I continued the ritual because this too lessened pain, and was, in its very poignancy, a consolation.

Writing of his life after his wife's death after fifty-one years of marriage, a widower told me:

When I am making my bed in the morning – something Anne normally did – I remember Anne, whilst ill in bed here four weeks ago, telling me every day that I was not much of a hand at bed-making. Now, I think I am getting quite good, and I say, quite happily, to Anne – 'I'm not doing badly, am I?' And I make my bed before breakfast, as Anne did normally.

When I'm cooking in the kitchen and I suddenly remember that I have not put an apron on, I chide myself as I don it – 'Sorry darling, I forgot.' I try and remember to clean my shoes every morning, as she would want me to do, and I am rather lazy about that unless reminded! I make a point of telephoning and thanking people the next day for hospitality, as Anne always did. In my attitudes towards other people I try and think how Anne would have behaved in similar circumstances and I attempt to emulate her.

Similarly, Monica Dickens wrote that after watering the garden, she found herself coiling the hose as her husband did.

Roy used to drive me mad by being so meticulous about things like coiling the hose. In protest, I'd leave it tangled and snaking everywhere. Recently, after therapeutic hours in the garden, I found myself coiling the hose in shipshape style. I felt Roy very close. I realized that instead of thinking: 'Why isn't he here to do this or that?' I could think: 'What a good thing I learned from him how to do this!'

Bereavement purists may well condemn this kind of behaviour on the grounds that it is 'denial', a dirty word in the bereavement world. But who cares? Most likely the behaviour won't last for ever; it is an extremely useful way of cushioning pain while passing time; it is doing no one any harm and it is no more a sign of denial than the cuddly transitional object of a child who uses a piece of soft material as a comforting substitute for Mum when she's not around.

Dreams are another way of helping to integrate the experience of bereavement into our lives. Our subconscious can do sterling work on our behalf. Sometimes dreams are horrific; but at least we wake up from them having had our worst experiences while asleep rather than in real life; sometimes they're comforting. Edie's mother wrote: 'I had long dream talks with her and we did things together and sometimes they were so good and she'd be so like her old self that I'd wake up feeling good, like you do after a happy communication with someone.'

There are wonderfully manipulative pieces of mind-warp that can fool you into beginning to live again, too. Most of these go: 'We'd better go on living for his/her sake.' 'She wouldn't have liked us to be sad for ever.' By turning the act of starting to live again into a sacrifice for the dead ('I am only smiling and cracking jokes because the dead person would have liked me to, not because I really want to'), friends and relations of the dead person find they can sometimes jump-start themselves into re-existence.

Interviewed for *The Times* by Julia Llewellyn Smith, Anthony Misiolek, the father of a thirteen-year-old daughter killed in a crash on the M40, said:

> When the tragedy happened we were in the middle of rehearsals for a local pantomime company. I had a major comedy role. I thought, 'I can't do this now.' Then one or two sensible people told me Nicola would have wanted it. Going on stage was one of the hardest things I have had to do. At the end I felt proud that I had done it for Nicola. I hope she was out there somewhere, watching with her friends.

In *Man's Search for Meaning*, the great psychologist Viktor E. Frankl also cites sacrifice as a way of finding meaning in the pain of bereavement.

> Once an elderly practitioner consulted me because of his severe depression. He could not overcome the loss of his wife who had died two years before and whom he had loved above all else. Now how could I help him? What should I tell him? Well, I refrained from telling him anything but instead confronted him with the question, 'What would have happened, doctor, if you had died first, and your wife would have had to survive you?' 'Oh,' he said, 'for her this would have been terrible; how she would have suffered!' Whereupon I replied, 'You see, doctor, such a suffering has been spared her, and it was you who have spared her this suffering; but now, you have to pay for it by surviving and mourning her.' He said no word but shook my hand and calmly left my office. Suffering ceases to be

suffering in some way at the moment it finds a meaning, such as the meaning of a sacrifice.

Then there is the somewhat hardboiled view that once you have been hurt by a death, nothing can ever hurt you as much again. This works fine on paper, but it does seem to involve turning your heart into a block of ice. Otherwise, another death can hurt you again. And another. And anyway, in my experience, the pain of bereavement is a pain that is always alive. Bereavement belongs in the land of the undead. If it goes away, it is only sleeping. It can wake at any time and come and punish you, often years later.

This rather bitter view, however, is at odds with Daphne du Maurier's experience. In *Death and Widowhood* she ends:

As the months pass and the seasons change, something of tranquillity descends, and although the well-remembered footstep will not sound again, nor the voice call from the room beyond, there seems to be in the air an atmosphere of love, a living presence. I say this in no haunting sense, ghosts and phantoms are far from my mind. It is as though one shared, in some indefinable manner, the freedom and the peace, even at times the joy, of another world where there is no more pain ... When Christ the healer said, 'Blessed are they that mourn for they shall be comforted,' he must have meant just this. Later, if you go away, if you travel, even if you decide to make your home elsewhere, the spirit of tenderness, of love, will not desert you. You will find that it has become part of you, rising from within yourself; and because of it you are no longer fearful of loneliness, of the dark, because death, the last enemy, has been overcome.

This is good, rousing, comforting stuff, whether you identify with her feelings or not, and there is any amount of poetry and literature on the subject of death, from the crass to the sublime, and many people find great comfort in reading it. It may be fantastic, like the bizarre 'Gone from Sight':

What is dying? I am standing on the sea-shore. A ship in the bay lifts her anchor, spreads her white sails to the morning breeze and starts out upon the ocean. She is an object of beauty and strength, and I stand and watch her until she hangs like a speck of white cloud just where the sea and sky mingle with each other. Then someone at my side says, 'There, she's gone!' Gone where! Gone from sight, that is all. Just at that moment there are other eyes watching her coming and other souls taking up the glad shout: 'There, she's coming!' And that is dying.

Or it may be a comforting saying, like that of Mother Julian of Norwich, who reminded us that

He said not: thou shalt not be tempested, thou shalt not be assailed, thou shalt not be afflicted; but he said: thou shalt not be overcome.

My favourite was sent to me by a bereavement counsellor.

The hurt you are feeling now, in time, will bring you a new strength. I know that, in time, you will smile again and truly feel it, and that your laughter will be genuine. But until your pain has gone away, and your sadness has disappeared, don't feel you have to be strong. What you are feeling is real. Don't feel you are wrong if you want to cry. There are some roads in life that we must travel alone, even though we may be surrounded by people we love. Some things in life, such as what you are feeling now, can't be felt by anyone but you. But just remember that you are not alone: everyone who loves you is walking with you in spirit and will be there with you. You will find a new strength, a new peace and a new happiness – it just takes a little time.

Thoughts and poems that before a death you might have thought almost yukky, suddenly shed the curtains of their sentimentality and reveal great truths. Don't be put off by the dreadful title of the book *All in the End is Harvest* (it's a nice idea, but it just isn't harvest), but read it, stuffed as it is with the most wonderful pieces of poetry, psalms, diaries and prose, all about bereavement. And if you don't read, writing all your feelings down can pass the time in an extremely therapeutic way. 'I wrote a lot about my father when he died five years ago,' wrote Thomas Mallon in *A Book of One's Own*.

I had a very happy relationship with my father, but there were gaps in it, and I used my diary to fill in some of these gaps. Losing my father was terrible, but it became almost a good thing that there were things to wonder about, to get confused and regretful about. It gave me work to do, things to think about with an eye toward solving them or being content to let them rest, instead of just wishing he were still here.

Although this isn't a 'how-to' book, it would be a mistake to omit a few practical hints. Don't decide to clear out your loved one's things all at once. If you can, do a little bit at a time, even if it's only twenty minutes a day. If you attack it too soon, you may get rid of too much too quickly; too slowly and you are left like Miss Haversham, in a shrine to the past. If friends ask if they can do anything, ask them perhaps to ring you once a week for the next couple of months. Give them a specific task. They want to know. Or ask them, if you can't face cooking for yourself, if they could either deliver a meal to you, or ask you round once a week.

'A friend advised that I let my family look after me,' wrote Edie's mother.

She said I should help them by giving them the responsibility and opportunity to do as much for me as possible. This was so useful, because I'm naturally sort of dominant, and not only did I find that it helped the family but friends and neighbours as well.

Make no major decisions like getting married again, emigrating, moving, getting a pet, or, perhaps, even dealing with the will, until a year has passed.

Make sure the security on your home is completely watertight. When you are alone, you can wake up in panic. Don't drive just after the death. You are more likely to have small accidents. If you want to cry, listen to music; if you don't want to cry, don't.

Mary Stott advised:

> If you are bereft, accept that you have to trudge through each day as it comes, thankful when it is over and hoping for nothing better the next day or the day after. Remember that millions of others have been through this intolerable experience and survived, even if just now you yourself have no wish to survive. However unlikely it seems now, there may still be a point in going on living. So do what is asked of you, accept kindly meant invitations, summon all your strength to fight self-pity and do something preferably practical and undemanding, as soon as you have the strength and the willpower.

Never think that you have 'got over' a death. It is just at that moment that its memory will strike again. And don't get caught out by surprise when you suffer anniversary symptoms. Even if you have not marked down the date of your friend or loved one's death in your diary, sure as eggs, when it comes round the following year, you may well feel uncommonly blue. At the beginning of one November, E. M. Forster wrote in his diary:

> Last night, alone, I had a Satanic fit of rage against mother for her grumbling and fault finding, and figured a scene in which I swept the mantelpiece with my arm and then rushed out of the door or cut my throat. I was all red and trembling after. I write it down partly in the hope that I shall see its absurdity and so refuse it admittance again.

The following year he made a note on the opposite page to this entry: 'Discover, some months later, that Oct 31 is the anniversary of my father's death.'

Rebecca Abrams revealed to a friend that she was feeling a little sad because it was the anniversary of her father's death. Her friend replied: '"But that was years ago. You can't keep on feeling sad about it." It was my turn to be surprised – and annoyed. "I don't want to feel this way," I said. "I just do. I can't help it."'

It is usually a time of grief and anxiety. Lawrence Whistler wrote of how he felt on the anniversary of his wife's death:

> She died at the dead point of the year, a few days before Advent, which is the spiritual beginning. On every 27th of November it seemed as if events were taking place again, almost as if they were branded on a portion of space which the earth passes through at that period. As the short day closed in, often with the same damp inertia, I felt that she was dying again, and again might be saved, and I was not at peace until a little after five in the evening.

But Goronwy Rees wrote in a letter to a friend that the anniversary wasn't as bad as he had anticipated.

> I have dreaded this Anniversary and had wondered how I could get through it, or what devices I could think of to avoid it. But life is so strange that somehow it has turned out happily for me, in that I have never been so intensely aware of Margie's presence, so grateful that all her terrible suffering was over, or so aware of her beside me, telling me that I must not grieve and that somehow, somewhere, she will always be with me.

Some people, rather than avoid the anniversary of a loved one's death, make a special point of remembering it, even celebrating their birthday, or their wedding anniversary. The ritual serves two purposes: to try to bring some of the memory of the dead person back to life; and to make a focus for grief, a focus which stops it building up and exploding at some other, less organized, time.

A book on bereavement is difficult to end because there is no ending to it. There is always another anniversary; the pain is always present. It never ends. I wish I could, like so many other books on bereavement, end on a consoling and comforting note and not a howling draught of reality. I wish I could say that 'This, too, will pass' and mean it. But however many endings I write, whenever I cast them in a comforting light, or add any hint about acceptance, or the cycle of life, I feel sick and ashamed of myself. I'm lying. I was glad to read Freud, who wrote this to his friend Binswanger:

> We find a place for what we lose. Although we know that after such a loss the acute stage of mourning will subside, we also know that we shall remain inconsolable and will never find a substitute. No matter what may fill the gap, even if it be filled completely, it nevertheless remains something else.

Bereavement is a rite of passage. Death has to happen. Death *does* happen.

And now, as the end of this chapter marks the end of this book, I find myself presented with yet another kind of personal dilemma. Even if I do find the right way of ending it, I can't bear to print it out. Why? Possibly because I'm incapable of letting my own feelings of bereavement out. Perhaps I am hanging on to them because they are all I have, a painful thought in itself. Perhaps because, since they are all I have, I am jealous of sharing them with others. Possibly, too, because by printing out this book I feel I am perpetrating a lie to myself – and to you. That I am saying: 'Ah, the bereavement book is over,' and making the corollary that the feelings of bereavement are over, too. A book on bereavement should never end because bereavement itself never ends. You never get over a death. It's with you always, a scar like a brand that will never fade. Unless you are an exceptionally spiritual person, I doubt if you will ever come to terms with it, either. The very best that most of us can do is to live with it. On and on and on and on . . . until we die ourselves, when the feelings of pain, anger and confusion will be handed on, a legacy of truth, to someone else to bear.

Postscript

I started this book eighteen months after my father died. I finished it eighteen months after that. It is now nearly three years since his death – and looking back, yes, of course it was 'too soon' to write about it. Funnily enough, it is *still* 'too soon' to write about it, because as I kiss the manuscript goodbye, yet more feelings bubble up, of excruciating grief and loneliness, of a kind I don't think I felt before. Or did I? I'm still a reluctant émigrée in a foreign country in which I don't know the language, and I miss my country of origin. True, it was a relief to get some feelings off my chest and rage about death generally, to call out to other people through the pages of this book: 'Do you feel like this?' 'Did you feel like this?' 'I'm not different, am I?' 'These feelings are normal, despite what everyone says, aren't they?' But even those who know me on the outside, people who know me quite well, probably will never know quite how tumultuous and changed is my inner reality.

What is amazing is that people are bereaved every day. Bereaved traffic wardens go to work and carry on traffic wardening; bereaved accountants go to work and carry on adding up figures – they may add them up again and again and make some mistakes, but they still get the job done. What is astonishing is the strength of the human spirit, that we still plod on, despite being shaken by the most powerful emotions we will ever experience. I have not missed – and am still not missing – a single piece of work, or a single appointment; I have not entertained more or less than before; like everyone else who is bereaved, I struggle on (some of the time on automatic pilot, admittedly) and here I am, I'm still alive. Well, sort of.

Everyone says to give it another couple of years and things may start to improve. But another couple of years! It seems like a lifetime. Don't they know that I'm getting *bored* with living on this kind of hectic, morbid, rollercoaster? I hardly know which from what any more, I'm so dizzy. I'm even reconsidering every-thing I said before, again and again. Nothing rings true; all my certainty is gone. Maybe grief *is* like a butterfly and I'm still in the cocoon. Maybe (though I can hardly believe I am writing this after everything I've said before) my father's death might not just be a merciful release for him, but a merciful emotional release for me, too, in the end.

I'm impatient to discover whether I have to live in this land of grief and rage and confusion for ever, or whether bereave-ment is actually a journey, and the boat is heading for another port. If so, I just hope it's a less smelly place than the port I'm in now.

I have to say, too, that just at this precise moment (and it will all change in a couple of hours, no doubt) I feel that since it can't possibly be worse, I suppose it can only be better. And although it might well be a mirage, as so many of my feelings have been, in the last month I *have* occasionally seen enough blue sky to make a sailor a pair of trousers. It'll rain tomorrow. Cloud over. But I did see that patch of sky. I *did*.

Well, I thought I did.

Addresses

I have placed Cruse at the top of this list because of its preeminence in the field. Other organizations appear in alphabetical order.

Cruse
Cruse House
126 Sheen Road
Richmond
Surrey TW9 1UR
Helpline: 0181–332 7227 (speak directly to a counsellor)
National organization for all bereaved people, which offers a service of counselling by trained people, a Parents' Circle (group counselling for the widowed parent with dependent children), advice on practical problems, and opportunities for social contact.

Carers' National Association
20–25 Glasshouse Yard
London EC1A 4JS
Helpline: 0171–490 8898
This organization aims to offer practical help and advice to anyone looking after an elderly relative and also provides bereavement counselling.

The Compassionate Friends
53 North Street
Bristol BS3 1EN
Helpline: 0117 9665 202
A compassionate self-help organization of parents whose child of any age, including adults, has died from any cause. Range of leaflets, newsletter. Offers befriending, not counselling.

The Cot Death Society
1 Browning Close
Thatcham
Newbury
Berkshire RG18 3EF
Helpline: 01635 861771

Foundation for the Study of Infant Deaths
14 Halkin Street
London SW1X 7DP
Helpline: 0171–235 1721
This organization is particularly concerned and interested in research into cot deaths. There are groups around the country. Counselling for parents bereaved in this way is provided, or parents can be put in touch with each other for mutual support.

Lesbian and Gay Bereavement Project
Vaughan M. Williams Centre
Colindale Hospital
London NW9 5HG
Helpline: 0181–455 8894

The London Association of Bereavement Services
356 Holloway Road
London N7 6PN
Tel: 0171–700 8134
Same as **The National Association of Bereavement Services** but for London area only.

Memorials by Artists
Snape Priory
Saxmundham
Suffolk IP17 1SA
Tel: 01728 688934
Nationwide service to provide fine hand-carved memorials designed by experienced artists.

The Miscarriage Association
Clayton Hospital
Northgate
Wakefield WF1 3JS
Helpline: 01924 200799
Gives information, help and support after a miscarriage. For information pack, enclose large s.a.e.

The National Association of Bereavement Services
20 Norton Folgate
London E1 6DB
Helpline: 0171–247 1080
An umbrella organization that can suggest help for those bereaved by the whole spectrum of deaths – from personal, natural deaths to post-disaster counselling.

Natural Death Centre
20 Heber Road
London NW2 6AA
Tel: 0181–208 2853
Will give information on all aspects of death, including DIY funerals. Send six first-class stamps for an information pack.

The Stillbirth and Neonatal Death Society (SANDS)
28 Portland Place
London W1N 4DE
Helpline: 0171–436 5881
Self-help organization for those who have had stillborn babies. They befriend, not counsel. National network of groups and contacts throughout the country.

Sources and Further Reading

You may wonder why I've recommended a few of the books below when I may have criticized some of their authors' attitudes in this book. The truth is that nearly every book on bereavement contains some kernels of wisdom, and since one man's bereavement book is his salvation and another his irritant, I can't tell which ones you'll enjoy. But there is something, however small, in all these books that should help every bereaved person.

Rebecca Abrams, *When Parents Die*, New Holland Publishing, 1992

Rosa Ainley (ed.), *Death of a Mother: Daughters' Stories* (various authors), Pandora, 1994

Diana Ajajan (ed.), *The Day My Father Died* (various authors), Running Press, 1994

Nicola Beauman, *Morgan: A Biography of E. M. Forster*, Hodder & Stoughton, 1993

Jeffrey Bernard, *More Low Life*, Pan, 1989

Ursula Bowlby, *Reactions to the Death of my Husband*, Bereavement Care, 1991; 10, No. 1: 5

Dr Robert Buckman, *I Don't Know What to Say: How to Help and Support Someone Who Is Dying*, Papermac, 1988

Maggie Callanan and Patricia Kelley, *Final Gifts: Understanding and Helping the Dying*, Hodder & Stoughton, 1992

Maria Cantacuzino, *Till Break of Day: Meeting the Challenge of HIV and AIDS at London Lighthouse*, Heinemann, 1993

Elizabeth Collick, *Through Grief: The Bereavement Journey*, Darton, Longman and Todd/Cruse, 1986

Roger Cooper, *Death Plus Ten Years*, HarperCollins, 1993

Monica Dickens, quoted with permission from the January 1987 *Reader's Digest*, Copyright © 1987 The Reader's Digest Association Ltd

Daphne du Maurier, *Death and Widowhood*, Cruse Publications

Father's Place, by a widow, Cruse Publications

Viktor E. Frankl, *Man's Search for Meaning*, Hodder & Stoughton, 1962

Kahlil Gibran, *The Prophet*, Heinemann, 1964

Dr Rosemary Gordon, *Growth Through Loss: A Jungian View of Loss*, Cruse Academic Papers No. 4, 1985

Joyce Grenfell, *Joyce: By Herself and Her Friends*, Macmillan, 1980

Susan Hill, *In the Springtime of the Year*, Hamish Hamilton, 1974

Susan Hill, *Personal Experiences of Bereavement*, Bereavement Care, 1988; 7, No. 3: 29–33

Sandra Horn, *Coping with Bereavement*, Thorsons, 1989

Elizabeth Jennings, *Collected Poems*, Macmillan, 1967

Jill Krementz, *How It Feels When a Parent Dies*, Gollancz, 1983

Elisabeth Kubler-Ross, *On Death and Dying*, Routledge, 1970

Harold S. Kushner, *When Bad Things Happen to Good People*, Pan, 1981

Tony Lake, *Living with Grief*, Sheldon Press, 1984

Christopher Leach, *Letters to a Younger Son*, Dent, 1981

Carol Lee, *Good Grief*, Fourth Estate, 1994

C. S. Lewis, *A Grief Observed*, Faber and Faber, 1961

Thomas Mallon, *A Book of One's Own*, Picador, 1984

Isaac Marks, *Living with Fear*, McGraw Hill, 1978

Georgina Monckton, *Dear Isobel*, Vermilion, 1994

Bob Monkhouse, *Crying with Laughter*, Century, 1993

Geoffrey Moorhouse, *OM – An Indian Pilgrimage*, Hodder & Stoughton, 1993

Blake Morrison, *And When Did You Last See Your Father?*, Granta Books, 1993

Iris Murdoch, *Metaphysics and Morals*, Chatto & Windus, 1992

Sherwin B. Nuland, *How We Die*, Chatto & Windus, 1994

Revd 'Seye Olumide, BA, MSc, *The Unexpected Death of Children through Disaster – a Personal View*, Cruse Publications, reprinted from *Hospital Chaplain*, March 1988

On the Death of a Parent (various authors), Virago, 1994

Colin Murray Parkes, *Bereavement: Studies of Grief in Adult Life*, Penguin, 1975

Colin Parry, *Tim – An Ordinary Boy*, Hodder & Stoughton, 1994

Frances Partridge, *Hanging On: The Diaries of Frances Partridge*, HarperCollins, 1990

Frances Partridge, *Other People: The Diaries of Frances Partridge*, HarperCollins, 1993

Lily Pincus, *Death and the Family*, Faber and Faber, 1976

Professor Brice Pitt, *Down with Gloom!*, Gaskell, 1993

Susan Poidevin, *Coming Through*, Cruse Publications, 1986

Beverley Raphael, *The Anatomy of Bereavement: A Handbook for the Caring Professions*, Routledge, 1984

Jenny Rees, *Looking for Mr Nobody: The Secret Life of Goronwy Rees*, Weidenfeld & Nicolson, 1994

Rosamond Richardson, *Talking About Bereavement*, Vermilion, 1991

Philip Roth, *Patrimony*, Jonathan Cape, 1991

James Saunders, *Next Time I'll Sing to You*, Heinemann, 1965

Vernon Scannell, *Collected Poems 1950–1993*, Robson Books, 1994

Edith Sitwell, *Collected Poems*, Macmillan, 1957

Carol Staudacher, *Beyond Grief*, Souvenir Press, 1988

Mary Stott, *Ageing for Beginners*, Basil Blackwood, 1981

Judy Tatelbaum, *The Courage to Grieve: Creative Living, Recovery and Growth through Grief*, Heinemann, 1981

Michael Tolkin, *Among the Dead*, Faber and Faber, 1993

L. N. Tolstoy, *The Death of Ivan Ilyich*, Penguin, 1960

Albert Torrie, *When Children Grieve*, Cruse Publications, 1978

Jill Tweedie, *Eating Children*, Viking, 1993

Susan Wallbank, *The Empty Bed*, Darton, Longman & Todd, 1992

Susan Wallbank, *Facing Grief: Bereavement and the Young Adult*, Lutterworth, 1991

Barbara Ward, *Healing Grief*, Vermilion, 1993

Evelyn Waugh, *Work Suspended*, Penguin, 1992

Alison Wertheimer, *A Special Scar: the Experience of People Bereaved by Suicide*, Routledge, 1991

Lawrence Whistler, *The Initials in the Heart*, Weidenfeld & Nicolson, 1987

Agnes Whitaker (ed.), *All in the End is Harvest: An Anthology for Those Who Grieve*, Darton, Longman & Todd, 1984

Dr R. M. Youngson, *Grief: Rebuilding your Life after Bereavement*, David & Charles, 1989